KICK THE DRINK... EASILY!

JASON VALE

KICK THE DRINK... EASILY!

Crown House Publishing Ltd
www.crownhouse.co.uk
www.crownhousepublishing.com

First published by
Crown House Publishing Ltd
Crown Buildings, Bancyfelin, Carmarthen, Wales, SA33 5ND, UK
www.crownhouse.co.uk
and
Crown House Publishing Company LLC
PO Box 2223, Williston VT 05495, USA
www.crownhousepublishing.com

First published 2011. Reprinted 2011 (twice), 2012, 2013 (twice),
2014, 2015, 2016 (twice), 2017 (twice), 2018, 2019.

Originally published as *Stop Drinking 4 Life, Easily!*
(Original ISBN: 0954766407)

British Library of Cataloguing-in-Publication Data. A catalogue
entry for this book is available from the British Library.

Print ISBN 978-184590390-9
Mobi ISBN 978-184590712-9
ePub ISBN 978-184590713-6

LCCN 2009936662

Edited by Fiona Spencer Thomas

Printed and bound in the UK by
TJ International, Padstow, Cornwall

A Special Dedication to …
My Beautiful Mother

While I was in the process of updating this book, my beautiful mother passed away. It is impossible to convey in words what this amazing woman meant to me and the void left by her departure. Having no brothers, sisters or a father, my mother was much more than simply my Mum or a great friend. What my mother did leave was a clear message to me – keep doing whatever you can to help lift people from their addictions, as well as always telling me, 'turn your lemons into lemonade.'

My mother always taught me that if you can help just one person then it has all been worth it. So here is the updated version of this book, designed to help just one person. I sincerely hope that person is you.

I love you Mum and I miss you every single day.

Contents

Please read
before you start ...

These days I am better known for my books on juicing and nutrition but what many people aren't aware of is that my first book was in fact the one you are holding right now.

I first wrote and self-published this book in 1999 when I was working as a therapist at an Allen Carr clinic (not Alan Carr the comedian, but Allen Carr the stop smoking 'guru'). I was fascinated by addiction, having been addicted to many drugs and indeed certain 'foods' myself, and wanted to help people set themselves free using any means at my disposal. After stopping drinking myself I wanted to write a book explaining just how easy it could be if you went about it the right way. This is the book you are reading now. I wish to point out that I wrote this book a full two years before Allen wrote his book entitled *The Easy Way To Control Alcohol*. The reason I mention this is because a couple of people wrote reviews saying my book is similar to Allen's book on alcohol and were, I think, insinuating that I had read his book on alcohol and then decided to write a similar one. This, to put the record straight, is not the case but I do not wish to go into the story of Allen Carr and myself here, as it would serve no purpose at all. Unfortunately Allen passed away a couple of years ago but I am pleased to say we connected once again before he died and we managed to put any disagreements behind us, acknowledging that the goal was simply to help others to freedom, not to have a competition about who wrote what first and which book is the best for the job. I really do not care which book, App or clinic works as long as it works. Everyone is different and some prefer the approach and style of one person over another, which is why it is vital to have as many books on this subject, and as many different approaches to it as possible, in order to set as many people free as possible.

Although I wrote this book over a decade ago, it has taken this long to get it officially published. However, despite the fact that it was not available in any bookshops, word spread and, over the years, the book has had several print runs. It has helped thousands of people free themselves of the addiction to what is the most widely used legal drug in the world and I have yet to meet anyone who has read the book and not changed his or her relationship with alcohol at least to some degree. This is evidence that the message in the original version works, so the new, fully updated version has, in essence, changed little from the original edition. This means there are a few old references, but the book worked so well I didn't wish to change it that much.

Having said that, many things have changed over the last ten years with regard to alcohol. One of the biggest changes was of course the crazy decision of the government of the time to bring in twenty-four-hour drinking in the UK. They believed, in their ignorance, that this would somehow help with alcohol related crime. Of course it didn't. What a shocker!

The other major change has been in the perception of alcohol. Although it still remains the only drug on earth you have to justify *not* taking, there are more and more people opening their eyes to the realities of this liquid drug. Just as smoking has seen an incredible paradigm shift over the past twenty years, I believe we are on the verge of a similar shift in attitudes to alcohol. There doesn't appear to be a week that passes by where alcohol related social problems aren't reported. More and more we see front-page headlines about 'Booze Britain' and how so many people are exceeding the recommended 'units.'

Over 90 per cent of the UK's population at one time smoked something containing tobacco and that figure is now below 30 per cent. As I write the updated version of this book, around 80 per cent of the UK's adult population still drinks alcohol but when I first wrote this book the figure was over 90 per cent. With the help of *Kick the Drink ... Easily* and other books like it, I feel we are on the brink of reducing incidences of excessive drinking and mass addiction as happened with smoking. It may take time but I am sure it will happen.

The approach I use is not for everyone as not everyone will agree with my views or the methodology. Similarly, not everyone will like the way I write, my language or the repetition in the book. However, if you allow yourself to be open and get past any prejudices you may have about the tone and my views on conventional treatment for those who want to stop drinking, you will find this book incredibly useful and, more importantly, effective.

If you are reading this page, I feel it is safe to say you do so because you wish to change your relationship with alcohol to some extent at least. If this is your goal, let your mind be free and relaxed while reading it. As I say with all my books, I write but I am not an author. I will never win a literary award and I don't have an Oxbridge education. What I do have is an incredibly simple way for you to understand the nature of the trap you are in and a ridiculously easy route out if you choose to take it. Please make a point of reading the short selection of testimonials taken from many who have used this approach before reading the book.

I love to hear from people who have benefitted from the book. Please feel free to write to me at the email address at the end but if, for whatever reason, the book doesn't have the desired effect, you may be interested to know that I still run alcohol sessions at my Ultimate Mind and Body Retreats in Turkey.

I wish you well on your journey.

Jason Vale

What People Say ...

This is an excellent book. I didn't feel a compulsion to give up alcohol when I started reading it. I only read it really because I have several of Jason Vale's books and was interested to hear what he had to say on this subject.

Before reading this book I would have described myself as a social drinker (a glass or two of wine most nights, lots more on a big night), although I have drunk significantly less than I used to over the last four years, having been either pregnant or breastfeeding two children! My main motivation for reading it was to lose weight by cutting down on alcohol.

However, I was fascinated by Jason's assertion that there is no such thing as an alcoholic and that everyone who drinks alcohol is an alcohol addict. Jason challenges the way that we view alcohol and the way that many people who consider themselves to be in control of their drinking simply aren't. As Jason points out, if someone said that they only eat bananas after midday, they only eat so many a week and limit overdosing on bananas to the weekend you would surely assume that they have a problem with bananas so why not with alcohol? As over 90 per cent of the population drinks alcohol it is considered normal and we assume that anyone who is teetotal is not normal or must have had a problem in the past.

Jason finds ways to challenge many of our long held perceptions or beliefs about alcohol. As I said earlier, I had no intention of giving up alcohol altogether when I started reading but, since finishing the book, I find that the last drink I had was on New Year's Eve and I have had absolutely no desire to touch a drop since. I have been to a couple of dinner parties and a black tie event since then; occasions where previously not drinking would have been inconceivable. My husband is incredulous, as are most of my friends. I must stress, I do not feel as though I am missing out being on the wagon; I simply do not want to drink and feel absolutely free of all the control I had to exercise in the past (i.e. I won't have one till Friday, won't have more than a quarter of a bottle of wine, etc.). That's all gone. It's an amazing book – open your mind!

Rachel

I haven't quite finished reading this book but it has already stopped me drinking. I can't see any reason why I would want to drink any longer. Jason gives very compelling reasons why drinking is not a good thing and the damage it actually does to your body and mind and why most people who drink don't think that they are actually addicted. Great reading, written in Jason's usual, fun style, it has changed my total perspective on alcohol, even though I wasn't thinking of giving up totally when I bought this book. I just wanted to cut down. Now I realise that it is very difficult to do this and that I would be better off just stopping and not giving in to this drug at all! Thanks Jase, you have changed my life!

Julie M

This book will definitely free you from having to put alcohol in your body ... If only everyone would read it, our society would be transformed for the better. It deserves to sell more copies than any other book ever written! If you need to cut down or stop drinking then look no further. This is the book you need.

James M

I think I was like many people out there who enjoyed the odd drink, but found that the odd one was becoming a daily routine. Either socially or alone I was becoming reliant on a bottle or two of wine a day. I managed to get hold of Jason's book and cannot believe that I have not or wanted to have a drink for over a week now (I know this seems a tad feeble but believe me, it's a huge step in my world). I even had a dream last night that I did have a drink and was truly upset that I had succumbed but, on awakening, I realised it was just a dream and felt joyous once again. I have felt so much healthier, aware and alive (not just hazing through each day!). I would recommend this book to anyone who realises that booze is having an adverse effect on your life and well-being. Thank you Jason.

Mrs K. D. Wooldridge

It's difficult to know exactly where to start, so I guess simplest is best:

THANK YOU.

It seems such a small word for what you've helped me achieve – TOTAL FREEDOM from alcohol. I had for quite some time (a few years if I am honest) before I read your book started to suspect that I was an alcoholic in the understood sense and I was terrified of all the implications that went with it, i.e.:

the 'fact' that it is an incurable illness;

the 'fact' that you have to take one day at a time and decide not to drink today;

the 'fact' that you are vulnerable for the rest of your life.

Thanks to your enlightened way of thinking I can now see how wrong the 'experts' are and how, although there are many whose lives have been saved by AA and other such organisations, these tormented souls live every moment of every day in fear. Whereas with your way I really do live Life In Fearless Excitement. I am proud to be in the real world and the real me (not the alcohol soaked version) is there to enjoy all of it.

There are home truths in your book which felt as though you had found my own personal life script and were exposing them, not with contempt or in order to shame, but with a gentle thought-provoking persuasiveness which enabled me, and I know will help anyone who drinks, to get free. Thanks again.

Angela

There is No Such Thing as an Alcoholic

For many people reading the first page of this book, the statement 'There is No Such Thing as an Alcoholic' may seem incredible or certainly difficult to accept, particularly if you have been labelled an 'alcoholic.' However controversial, I intend to prove without any doubt that there is no such thing as an alcoholic, as society understands it, and that there is no such disease as alcoholism.

I would like to take you on a journey to discover the truth behind the most used and generally accepted drug in the world. It is time for us all to take our heads out of the sand and finally to face up to the truth about alcohol. Alcohol addiction has never been seen for what it really is as the subject of a drink problem and the possibility of a person being addicted to alcohol are rarely addressed or all too often swept under the carpet. We have been conditioned to believe that you are either a 'normal' drinker or that you have lost control and are an 'alcoholic.' As a result, people who have finally woken up to the fact that they are not in control have to keep quiet about it for fear of being made an outcast. If they are brave enough to voice a desire to stop drinking, they are called alcoholics which suggests they have an incurable disease and would have to 'give up' drinking forever. This is an unwelcome and frightening thought for anybody who drinks.

The truth is that is the vast majority of people are never in genuine control of their alcohol intake as I will attempt to prove beyond doubt in this book. With any other form of drug addiction, the addict who wants to quit is applauded for realising that they were never in control but the alcohol addict is given a label and made to feel inferior. In reality the person who realises they are not in control is far from inferior. In fact, they are well ahead of the game. After all, you can only escape a trap when you know you are in one and the majority of people who drink alcohol have no idea that they are. It is one of the subtlest traps ever devised and one that has fooled millions for generations.

> You can only escape a trap when you know you are in one.

Alcohol has always been seen as very different from any other form of drug taking; so much so that drinking alcohol is rarely described as drug taking at all. But, for a significant majority, drug taking it is and drug addiction it is. What is more, it is the only drug in the world where, when you stop taking it, you are seen as having a problem.

> ... it is the only drug in the world where, when you stop taking it, you are seen as having a problem.

As you read this book, you will soon begin to realise that alcohol addiction is exactly the same as any other drug addiction. It will become clear that the amount people drink has very little to do with their genes, character or personality. You will realise that the only difference between alcohol and all other drugs is the conditioning and brainwashing that we have been subjected to from a very early stage. This book will be much more than a simple eye opener and will change the way you see alcohol forever. It will show you not only how to stop drinking, should you choose to, but how you will enjoy the process and enjoy your life so much more without having to drink alcohol. I will also show you why nobody ever needs alcohol and that all the reasons given for drinking are part of one of the most ingenious confidence tricks ever to dupe mankind.

They say you can fool some of the people some of the time but not all the people all of the time. However, I believe that is exactly what alcohol has done. We have all been conned into believing there are genuine benefits to drinking alcohol. Many of you will be convinced that this is the case. However, I would like a chance to prove that there are no genuine benefits whatsoever. I do not expect you to accept or believe what I say at this stage. After all, we all have thousands of references to back up our belief that there are good and bad aspects to alcohol. Nonetheless, I would like you to turn a page in your mind, open it as wide as you possibly can, so that we can begin the process of removing years of conditioning and brainwashing. It is about time we all woke up to the truth and stopped kidding ourselves. Alcohol drinking is alcohol addiction and alcohol addiction is drug addiction and drug addiction is a form of disease which gets worse and worse – unless you cure it.

Now that I have your attention please let me introduce myself. My name is Jason Vale and I am a non-drinker. Now in case you start having images of a holier than thou non-drinker whose idea of a good night out is having a cup of cocoa while watching bowls, then you would be very much mistaken. Nor am I a person who hates alcohol drinkers, cannot socialise with them or wants to judge them in any way. Yes, I am a non-drinker but I am also a non-heroin addict and a non-crackhead but you wouldn't think any less of me for that and you certainly wouldn't pre-judge me for not taking heroin or crack. However, alcohol is seen very differently. It is the only drug that people will question you not taking.

> ... alcohol is seen very differently. It is the only drug that people will question you not taking.

Now to be fair, I have never been a heroin addict or a crackhead but, just so you fully understand where I am coming from, I have been a drinker. Well, not just a drinker believe me; I was no slouch when it came to drinking! I was a very heavy drinker and very badly hooked (or so I thought). I was, at one stage in my life, possibly one of the world's worst alcohol addicts you could ever meet. Even then I knew all the reasons why I shouldn't drink and at times I actually wished that I didn't need to drink. But what was my alternative? To become a non-drinker? To be honest that sounded like a disease in itself. I really wouldn't have wanted to suffer that as my life seemed bad enough as a drinker.

Even today I hate using the terms non-drinker or teetotaller because they have such negative connotations. That is why most of us pre-judge people who don't drink. I don't know about you but, when I was drinking and heard that someone was a non-drinker or had given up the booze, I immediately thought things along the lines of 'boring bastard'! I apologise for the language but one of my main fears about stopping drinking was the thought that I would turn into one of them. I believed that if I stopped drinking, I would be missing out. I thought I would feel deprived of the wonderful pleasures of alcohol; the calming effect, the relaxation, the sociable aspect of having a few beers with the lads or a bottle of wine with dinner. The warm glow of a brandy, the crisp bite of a glass of chilled white wine, the hot toddy, the banter, the chatter, the laughter, the fun all added up to my idea of a good time. In short, if

I stopped drinking altogether, I would no longer have a life. Until, that is, I realised it was all nonsense.

I am pleased to say that stopping drinking certainly hasn't turned me into a bore or a social hermit. On the contrary, it has enhanced my social life and given me back my courage, confidence and a quality of life that I had forgotten even existed. I am now in full control of my drinking for the first time in my adult life. I now drink as much as I want, as often as I want and whenever I want to. I no longer have to exercise willpower, self-discipline and control to avoid drinking too much. Every single day I have the quantity of drink I choose without worrying about work, what people will think of me or even how I am going to feel. That is true control.

The reason why I have such control now is because I do not drink alcohol any more. Not because I cannot drink it but because I just don't want to. Of course I could drink alcohol whenever I want and there is nothing stopping me. I simply have no desire to do so.

A few years ago I would have thought that impossible. Me, a non-drinker? Never! I could not imagine what life would be like without alcohol. I didn't even want to contemplate the idea of never drinking again. The mere thought of stopping altogether would be far too scary even to consider. Who would want to spend the rest of their life without drink? Not me! Whenever I started to realise that I was drinking a little too much, I would look for ways to exercise more control over my drinking without having to stop completely. I would think of ways to cut down and all the different methods of reducing my intake including going 'on the wagon' and abstaining for a while or making every other drink a soft one. I would drink water with alcohol to reduce the dehydration or even discipline myself not to go out on certain nights to help reduce my intake. But to stop altogether for the rest of my life? Never.

I once managed to go on the wagon for three months. It was one of the worst periods of my life. I felt miserable and deprived and stayed in most of the time. I thought, what is the point of going out to a social gathering if I am not drinking? How can you possibly enjoy yourself at a get-together without alcohol?

I have been a non-drinker for over ten years now and it has been without question the best ten years of my life. I have never once missed alcohol since I stopped and now socialise more than ever before. I do not feel miserable and depressed when I am not drinking because there is nothing to feel miserable about. In fact, I feel elated to be free from what was a constant struggle to gain control. I feel so relieved to be mentally and physically free.

So just how badly addicted was I? When I was in my late teens I would get through sixteen pints of lager every day. At weekends I would drink even more. Sometimes I would even drink Special Brew and Thunderbird for breakfast! This went on for a couple of years and I was warned that I might be an alcoholic. Personally, I did not think I was. After all, I was only enjoying a drink just like everybody else, only I drank a little more than most. However, the more people told me I was drinking too much, the more conscious I became of it. At this stage you may agree that I was an alcoholic as such is the power of social conditioning. After all, if you drink in the morning, you must be.

One day I decided that enough was enough and I had to reduce my intake. This should have been impossible were I an alcoholic. After all, that is the difference isn't it? Drinkers are in control and alcoholics are out of control. I went from being what society would call an alcoholic to being a normal drinker. This obviously meant that I wasn't an alcoholic after all and didn't really have a problem as I was now back in control because if you are in control, there is no problem. I made a point of only drinking at weekends. Oh, and at birthday parties. Oh yes, and at weddings and restaurants, not to mention Easter, Christmas, New Year, christenings, as well as holidays, barbecues, parties and any social events. I would drink when watching the football, drink to relieve stress, to help me calm down and relax after a hard day. I would drink with meals, the odd glass of wine in the bath, not forgetting the ones for a little 'Dutch courage.' As you see, I only drank as 'little' as any other normal drinker who is in control.

Was I ever really choosing to drink on these occasions or did I have to in order to have a good time? Had my freedom of choice already been taken from me? It was this thought that led me to question whether I even wanted to be in control. I started to realise that I was using some degree of willpower and discipline on a weekly, if not daily, basis to avoid drinking too much. Did this mean that I was in control of my alcohol intake because I could apparently control it at times or did it simply mean that I was in a constant battle to gain control? I started to ask myself 'if you consciously have be in control to make sure you don't drink too much, then surely you cannot really be in control?' I now realise that I was never actually in full control of my alcohol intake and that very few people who drink alcohol are ever really in control.

YOU CANNOT HAVE FREEDOM OF CHOICE WITHOUT THE FREEDOM TO REFUSE.

For the first time since just before I started drinking, I now have full control once more. The reason is because I no longer have to exercise willpower. It is the having to exercise control that proves the addict is not in control. I will repeat this point as I believe it to be a vital one. You cannot have freedom of choice without the freedom to also refuse.

Confused? I apologise. I'm racing ahead of myself. There is a lot of brainwashing and conditioning to be removed before you can even start to understand, let alone accept what I am saying. In fact some of my statements may be quite bewildering but all I ask while you read this book is that you open your mind as much as possible and come with me as we explore the myths about the most used and accepted drug addiction in the world.

Alcohol Addiction

You may be asking yourself at this stage what makes me, Jason Vale, so qualified to write such a book? What reasons should you have for acting on my advice, following my instructions or even listening to what I have to say? What qualifications do I have? What is my medical background? After all, there are many books written by ex-drinkers offering advice on how to give up. What makes me so different? Why should you follow my advice when I am not as medically or perhaps even as academically qualified as many of them?

The difference is that I am genuinely free! Yes, FREE. Let me be very clear on this point. I am not 'in recovery,' not missing out, not pining for drink or feeling deprived. I am not feeling miserable because I am not drinking, opting out of life, or attending sessions every week, and I haven't found religion. I mean that I am free, really FREE.

The freedom that I now enjoy and the mental tools that helped me achieve it are what make me so qualified to help all 'alcohol addicts' which I have now done for years. I read several books on how to stop drinking when I was a drinker but they contained diatribes and messages of doom and gloom. In fact, if non-drinkers were to read some of them it would probably have driven them to drink. Every single book was written either by an ex-alcoholic (their term, not mine) or by a doctor who was still a drinker. The ex-alcoholic would be complaining from the start, informing you from page one that you have an incurable disease and describing how you would have to spend the rest of your life in something called 'recovery.' It's hardly inspiring. As for the doctor or anyone giving advice on how to do something they haven't done themselves, it's hard to swallow. How can anybody offer advice on how to stop drinking when they are still drinking? It would be equivalent to *The Easy Way to Sparkling Wit and Repartee* by Gordon Brown. It just wouldn't wash. I realise you don't have to be the best football player in order to be a good coach but I do feel it helps if you can at least kick a ball.

We need to understand that, however well intentioned, many doctors belong to what I call the 'state the obvious' brigade when they pronounce: 'You're drinking too much. You really should cut down or perhaps stop altogether. Alcohol is killing you, destroying your life and causing you and your family all kinds of heartache.'

Telling the drinker what they are already fully aware of insults their intelligence. Imagine sinking in quicksand while somebody walks past saying, 'You should get out of there you know, you're sinking. Unless you get out you will probably die.' That sounds ridiculous I know, but it's no more ridiculous than the doctor who tells somebody who already knows that they are drinking too much. One of the times when a drinker will reach for a drink is when they feel under pressure or stressed out, so pressurising people to stop drinking usually has precisely the opposite effect.

I must emphasise that I am not condemning doctors who are in their profession to help people. Some may believe strongly that by listing the reasons might help someone quit or at least to cut down on their consumption. This approach may sound logical but, as you will discover in this book, everything about alcohol that appears logical is, in reality, the complete opposite. For example, Drinkline, at the time the first edition of this book was published, was considered to be one of the leading organisations offering expert help to those who want to stop drinking. They offer one recommendation which, on the surface sounds like good logical advice but is in fact the opposite: 'Note down all the reasons you can think of for stopping drinking.' If we question it for just a second, we soon discover that, because addiction is not logical, it is far from good advice. Listing all the reasons why you shouldn't drink will not make it easier for you to stop, just as writing down all the reasons why you shouldn't be in quicksand will not make it easier for you to stop sinking. Alcohol addicts already know all the reasons why they shouldn't drink. Bringing these facts into focus will not make it easier to stop and usually will have the opposite effect. Let me explain why.

ADDICTION ISN'T LOGICAL.

First, people who are in the advanced stages of alcohol addiction are constantly being pressured by loved ones, their doctors or society in general into stopping drinking, or at least cutting down their alcohol intake. All this does is cause resentment. Nobody likes being told what to do. The prospect of giving up immediately gives the drinker a feeling of self-sacrifice and a strong sense of deprivation. The more deprived they feel, the more they will want a drink. The more they want the drink, the more deprived they feel. It's a vicious circle.

Second, a common mistake that people make when they try to stop drinking is to focus on all the reasons why they should not drink. They come up with list after list of reasons why they should not be doing it, like health, money, children, family, hangovers, slavery to drinking and violence. Add to that the other reasons such as arguments, lethargy, weight and employment problems and so on, there are plenty.

Drinkers already know all the reasons why they should not drink. The truth is that people do not drink alcohol for these reasons but for what they feel are the positive benefits like the pleasure, as a crutch, to help them calm down, to relax, to give them confidence and courage, to make them happy and merry and so on.

Just so you know what is in store, this book is not going to be a long drawn out lecture on why people should not drink as you already know the reasons. This book will be very different from the usual 'doom and gloom' approach to giving up drinking. By this, I mean the approach where the horrors of drink are explained so the addict will hopefully stop out of fear. Once they have stopped they are then told that they are never really cured but will have to spend the rest of their lives in something called 'recovery.' No wonder they feel all doom and gloomy when they stop. So would I if I thought I would have to suffer forever and that freedom was unachievable.

Not only is freedom possible but it is also easy and extremely enjoyable to achieve. Once you understand fully how the confidence trick works, not only will you not envy people who drink but you will look at them as you might a heroin addict and genuinely pity them. I am fully aware that there will be many people reading this book who have lost a great deal, suffered greatly at the hands of alcohol and desperately need to stop. However, if that is you, you are not unique or alone. I have had best friends die because of alcohol. I have seen mental and physical abuse in my own family because of alcohol. I have had two family members literally drink their lives away, one in their prime at forty-nine. I have spent nights in prison because of alcohol. I have lost relationships because of alcohol. I have also lost jobs because of alcohol. I have watched friends and family suffer physically and mentally because of alcohol. I have seen people lose their eyes, literally, because of alcohol. I have seen people disfigured for life by broken bottles as a direct result of drinking. We all know the horror stories and, as you will discover, there is hardly anyone on this planet (in communities where drink is allowed) who hasn't been either directly or indirectly affected by the drug called alcohol.

FEAR KEEPS YOU DRINKING.

Despite my previous experience, I now hold the view that the past is the past and that, no matter what alcohol has done, it is now time to move on. I am also aware that there are many people reading this book who are not that desperate, have never really thought about stopping drinking forever and believe they are in control.

For years I never thought about stopping drinking for one reason and one reason alone – FEAR. As I have mentioned, the thought of never drinking again didn't just make me nervous, it petrified me. I now know that the majority of alcohol addicts are just as scared as I was and it is fear that actually keeps them hooked. Whether it's a drinker who is desperate to stop, or someone who just wants to stop because they are fed up with drinking, the fears are the same for everyone. It is only fear that prevents them from doing the very simple task of stopping drinking. It was not the physical withdrawal that scared me but the fear that I would never be able to enjoy or cope with my life in the same way again without alcohol. All kinds of ideas went through my mind when I thought 'I should give up drinking.' I would get butterflies in my stomach and my mind would race. I would think of every possible future scenario involving me and no alcohol. It was not a pretty picture. Every image was of me standing with a soft drink, feeling miserable and deprived. I feared that social occasions would never be the same again. I feared becoming an outcast. I felt that I wouldn't even want to go out if I couldn't drink. What would I do on my birthday? What about Christmas, New Year, holidays? The biggest fear I had was that the craving for alcohol would never go. I thought that I would forever have to use willpower and discipline not to drink. The truth was that I thought I wanted to stop drinking but I wanted to drink as well. That is why I was never sure if I really wanted to stop altogether. I was as confused as hell.

Since I stopped drinking I see very clearly that it is fear that prevents people from breaking free. Don't you have some of these fears too? Doesn't the thought of never having a drink again fill you with fear or maybe even complete and utter terror? Maybe you picked up this book just to 'cut down' and that sentence alone makes you want to shut the book and run! These fears keep people drinking and make them block their minds to the health, money, hangovers, slavery and the effects on their families and friends caused by drink.

However, what alcohol addicts fail to realise (and what I failed to realise a few years ago) is that all those fears are only caused by one thing and one thing alone: the alcohol itself. People who do not drink do not have these fears. Before you started drinking you did not have these fears and I no longer have these fears. I now want to scream from the rooftops and tell the world that they really do not need to drink alcohol; they just think they do. The need for alcohol is caused by alcohol and it's easy to stop once you realise that there are no genuine benefits to drinking the stuff and that life is infinitely better without it.

Come with me on an exciting journey to remove the brainwashing, conditioning and all the illusions surrounding the alcohol trap so that once you understand them fully, all your fears will be removed forever.

> ... remove the brainwashing, conditioning and all the illusions surrounding the alcohol trap ...

At this stage you may firmly believe that you do not want to become a non-drinker. I fully understand this. All I ask is that you read this book with an open mind and you just may start to think differently. You have nothing to lose. When I say an open mind, I mean really open, as wide as possible. A few years ago I would probably have dismissed most of this book. The only way your perception of the drug called alcohol can possibly change is if, just while you read this book, you put aside all your preconceptions. Forget everything you have ever been taught about alcohol. Forget everything your parents taught you, everything that your doctor told you and everything you have told yourself about alcohol. Most people believed that the world was flat at one stage; it took somebody with an open mind to see through that misconception and discover the truth. Once the illusions and brainwashing have been eliminated you will enjoy your life so much more without alcohol. I do not mean that you will be richer and healthier, simply that you will not miss drinking. You will have more courage and confidence and, far from having a void in your life when you stop, you will feel more fulfilled than you have felt in years. As impossible or daunting as that may sound at the moment, once you understand the nature of the trap, it would be hard to convince you otherwise. In fact it would be hard to persuade you to drink again.

However, there is so much brainwashing and conditioning to be removed before we reach that stage and in order for you to find your way out of the alcohol trap that you need to do a few things:

1.   Read this book with a very open mind.

2.   Read the whole book through; don't just dip in.

3.   Follow my 'Steps to Freedom.'

The first step is to continue drinking until you have finished reading this book. Now do let me make myself clear here. I don't mean get plastered every time you read the book! It just means do not attempt to stop drinking until all the brainwashing has been completely removed. If you had already stopped drinking before you picked up this book but don't feel free or still miss drinking and feel deprived, it will enable you to get truly free. However, if you have stopped already for a length of time then do not – I repeat – DO NOT start drinking again. Read the book with an open mind and your mental cravings will gradually be destroyed as you make your way through the chapters. If you are still drinking, then continue as normal until you have finished the book.

As you read, there may well be several points that make you see the light but please do not stop until you have completely finished as you need to have a full understanding of all the possible pitfalls. For this reason, perhaps the most important step of all is actually to finish the book. Do not let fear prevent you from completing it as it is time to break through your fears and find your freedom. Read at least a chapter a day to keep the momentum. It is so easy to start a book, but over 80 per cent of people who buy a 'self-help' book don't finish it.

Every point I make is for a reason to make absolutely certain that you succeed permanently. Success means freedom and freedom means not pining for a drink, not feeling deprived, not opting out of life and not getting angry or upset that you are not drinking ever again. If you read this book with your mind as open as the universe and follow my Steps to Freedom you will achieve what I have achieved:

TRUE FREEDOM FROM HAVING TO DRINK ALCOHOL.

You will find that some of the points in the book are repeated. I make no apologies for this at all. The message is very simple. Understanding the alcohol trap is simplicity itself but, in order for it to gel fully in your mind, some of the key fundamental points are repeated throughout the book almost as a form of hypnosis and they are repeated on purpose. We have a lot to get through so let's get started right away by removing a huge chunk of the brainwashing: the belief that if people are not alcoholics, then they are in control of their drinking. So, the first question that people ask themselves when they think they can no longer control their drinking is ...

Am I an Alcoholic?

The simple answer is no, you are not; never have been and never will be. The reason I know this is because, as mentioned already, there is no such thing as an alcoholic, as society understands it, and there is no such illness as alcoholism.

I realise that is a pretty bold and probably controversial statement to make but I assure you that it is an accurate one. In fact it's organisations like AA (Alcoholics Anonymous) that create the myth that there is a disease called alcoholism. I am more than aware that such a bold statement will make many of your hackles rise but please do not misread what I am saying. AA have without question saved the lives of thousands, if not millions, of people. The commitment, help and support they give to alcohol addicts around the world, around the clock, is beyond admirable. I also believe there will always be a need for organisations like AA as no one single approach works for everyone and not everyone will be in a position to take in fully the concept outlined in this book. So if you have been to AA or are still going, please, please do not misunderstand what I am saying. There will always be a need for such organisations and they will always save lives. No, the bone of contention I have with organisations like AA is that, however well intentioned their motives, they suggest that there is no cure for the disease known as alcoholism. By its own admission, AA has never cured a single alcoholic.

Try thinking of yourself as an alcoholic. You need help. So where do you go? Well, first of all you need to know for certain if you have the disease called alcoholism. The first thing you do is consult your doctor. Your physician cannot tell you if you are an alcoholic but may refer you to AA, Drinkline, Alcohol Concern or whatever specialist organisation happens to be at hand. Next, you phone one of these organisations to find out if you have the disease. The problem is that nobody can tell you if you are an alcoholic. AA, for example, simply states the following in one of their official booklets:

'If you repeatedly drink more than you intend or want to, or if you get into trouble when you drink, you may be an alcoholic. Only you can decide. No one in AA will tell you whether you are or not.'

So even AA, which claims to be the world's leading expert on coping with alcoholism, cannot tell you if you have a disease that they appear to have invented. So who can? Well, nobody apparently. Only you can decide. Now that does not exactly inspire me with confidence from the start. Only I can decide if I have this disease? 'They,' the people who created this 'alcoholism' disease, cannot tell me? So, if we do have to decide for ourselves, what guidelines do we have to go on? Well, according to AA if you regularly drink more than you intend or want to, or if you get into trouble when you are drunk, then you may be an alcoholic. Are they kidding? There isn't one person I know who drinks alcohol who doesn't repeatedly drink more than they intend. It's the nature of the drug. And as for getting into trouble when you have been drinking, hasn't everybody who drinks got into trouble at some point in their lives because of drink? Of course they have! So according to AA's official booklet, if we take their guidelines, everybody who drinks alcohol may be an alcoholic. That would mean that 80 per cent of the population the UK was born with a disease for which there is no known cure. I have only one thing to say to that.

BULLSHIT!

Did you know that alcoholism is now included in the same category as cancer and heart disease? Some claim it is inherited, that it's in your genes and there is nothing you can do about it. There are even people who claim they can tell if somebody is an alcoholic by the time they are TWO. Some people believe there are alcoholics who have never even touched a drop of alcohol in their lives. Yes, they actually believe there are people who have never drunk alcohol who have this disease. What I want you to do while reading this book is question this kind of rubbish. We end up believing it because we have been conditioned to accept it unquestioningly but, once you start to question, it just doesn't make sense. Do you believe that heroin addicts have a disease called heroinism or that they are heroinoholics? It's nothing to do with the drug, you understand, they were born with a disease called heroinism and can do nothing about it. Do you honestly believe that there are heroin addicts out there who have never taken heroin in their lives? Can you believe for a second that there are smokers who have never had a cigarette? Do you think you can tell whether someone will take crack cocaine by the time they are two years old? Do you honestly believe that you inherit these addictions or that they are in your genes? Do you believe that people who are addicted to chocolate were born with a disease which meant that they would have to eat chocolate all their lives and could do nothing about it? When you were two did you say, 'Thank God I can communicate properly as, now I can talk, I can ask for a drink. I've been gagging for one for two years'?

All I ask of you while you read this book is that you use your common sense and question this nonsense. I know that we have heard this stuff for years but just because it is put across by 'experts' does not make it the truth. Open your mind and use your own judgement to come to an intelligent conclusion. If you have been labelled an alcoholic yourself and it has become part of who you are, then I urge you to open your mind and ask how there can be any such thing as an alcoholic? It is time to see the truth. The word 'alcoholic' is just a name attached to people who realise they are hooked. It is time to get rid of this ridiculous label, because that is all it is – a label.

The fact is, regardless of what you may have been told, you are not an alcoholic, because there is no such thing. However, if the thought of being without alcohol fills you with fear, then you are an alcohol addict and you are hooked. So what's the difference? The difference is that there is an easy, straightforward cure for alcohol addiction and you're reading about it whereas, according to alcoholism's creators, there is no known cure for their disease.

In reality, people who drink alcohol regularly *and* fear being without it are in exactly the same position. They are all hooked. It doesn't matter if they only drink at weekends or whether they drink all day and every day. They are hooked and addicted to a drug called alcohol. It is easy to understand this addiction with other drugs. If somebody takes heroin, they are a heroin addict; if someone takes crack cocaine, they are a 'crackhead'; if somebody smokes, they are a nicotine addict. Would you change your view if the person taking heroin said: 'I'm not addicted to heroin; I'm in full control. I don't need it all the time. I can do without it. It's not like I take it all the time. I'll prove I don't have a problem with heroin. I only take it at weekends, on special occasions and if I'm feeling a bit stressed out. What's more, I cannot be addicted because I don't take heroin in the morning'? If you heard someone saying this would you think they were clearly not addicted and in full control of their heroin intake? Would you believe that they could take heroin whenever they liked without getting hooked? Or would you know for certain that they were already addicted and simply trying to justify the small quantities of the drug they were already taking?

I am not saying that everyone who drinks any amount of alcohol is hooked because clearly that is not the case. What I am saying, and I need this to be clear, is that anyone who fears life without alcohol and drinks on a regular basis is hooked. My definition of how to know if you are addicted to something or not is this:

> If the thought of never doing 'IT' again (whatever the IT is for you, in this case alcohol) fills you with fear, you are hooked; if it doesn't you aren't.

I like strawberries, no, I LOVE them but, if for whatever reason I had to stop eating them, it wouldn't fill me with fear. I would be disappointed but I wouldn't think I couldn't cope or enjoy life without them. That's the difference between 'I *choose* to' and 'I *have* to.'

It is so obvious with drugs like heroin and nicotine so why is it not the case with the drug alcohol? Why can't people see that they are addicted to alcohol? The reason why it isn't that evident is because almost 80 per cent of the UK population drinks alcohol according to the Insititute of Alcohol Studies. However, when it comes to any drug addition it is almost impossible to get the true figure as many people are, let's say, economical with the truth! I don't know about you, but my own research tells me the figure is probably over 90 per cent. However, even by their figures, if 80 per cent of the population took heroin if it were legal and we had always been conditioned to believe that shooting up was a natural social pastime, then it's possible that heroin taking would not be seen as drug addiction either. It is possible that we might actually believe that using heroin was normal. At the same time we need to remember that most people who offer advice on alcohol addiction take the drug themselves. They are the alcohol addicts and it is they who form the biggest sales force for the alcohol industry. After all, it was only the influence of other drinkers that got us into drinking in the first place. The illusions that alcohol creates simply confirm what we have been conditioned to believe by other drinkers.

So the poor drinker, even if he or she thinks s/he is drinking too much and has started to become conscious that s/he is not actually in control and wants to quit, is immediately labelled an 'alcoholic.' If you are not an alcoholic, what possible reason could you have for even wanting to stop? The drinker is then left in what they see as a no-win situation; either tell the world that they are not in control or lie about their intake and carry on drinking with their heads in the sand. The problem is that, unlike smoking where people can openly express a desire to stop, the drinker has to put up a front and lie, otherwise declare himself an alcoholic. What a choice. It is the only drug in the world that is differentiated in this way, depending on just how much of the drug is taken. What is the difference between normal drinking and alcoholism and at what point do you become an alcoholic? How much do you need to drink in a day to qualify for the title? How much heroin does a person have to take before they are hooked? When do you progress from heroin user to heroinoholic? How much cocaine do you need to take before you get the disease cocaineism? How many cigarettes do you need to smoke each day before you go from a normal or occasional smoker to smokeaholic?

People feel ashamed to admit that they have realised they are no longer in control and would like to stop drinking. *They* are seen as the problem and not the drug. With all other drug addictions it's the other way around. Many smokers say they want to stop yet they are never branded with an extraordinary title like nicotineaholic. The main problem is that, if you sense you are in trouble with alcohol, it is seen as your weakness rather than a result of the drug itself.

When I was growing up I remember seeing an advertisement featuring a heroin addict lying on a floor in a darkened room saying 'I can handle it.' It was on television all the time, 'I can handle it.' I remember thinking how pathetic that heroin addict looked and how ridiculous the remark sounded, yet I kept repeating the same nonsense when I was hooked on alcohol. It seemed normal to me. We have been brainwashed into believing that, either you are out of control with alcohol (which means that you are either a weak-willed jellyfish or probably an alcoholic), or you are in full control of what you are doing. What would you choose? I know which option I would rather choose. It's the one I chose for years. After all, who wants to admit they are out of control? This is the nonsense most drinkers spout: 'I can control my drinking. I might drink a bit too much on occasion but I am of course in control.' You see, apparently that is the difference between alcoholics and 'normal drinkers.' Alcoholics have lost control, whereas normal drinkers are in control.

> ... who wants to admit they are out of control?

RUBBISH!

Have you ever seen anybody who is drunk being in control of their actions? It is a contradiction in terms. And what is meant by 'normal drinker'? If I kept saying to you that I was in full control of my banana intake, that I only have them a few times week, I can take them or leave them, I have more at weekends but then, doesn't everybody? If I said that I can even go two complete days without bananas, wouldn't you immediately know that I had a problem with my bananas? Doesn't the mere fact that I am trying to justify how few I eat prove that the bananas are indeed controlling me? Doesn't it really mean that I have to exercise discipline to try and keep control of my intake? What I am saying is that, if I said this about my banana intake, I would have a problem and you would know it.

There are some experts who do not use the term 'alcoholic' and say that people who are not in control of their drinking have 'Alcohol Dependency Syndrome' or ADS but doesn't everybody who drinks alcohol regularly have Alcohol Dependency Syndrome? Don't all heroin addicts have 'Heroin Dependency Syndrome' or smokers 'Nicotine Dependency Syndrome'? What I mean is that anyone who drinks alcohol depends on it and feels they need it at certain times in order to cope, or enjoy themselves. Clearly, a dependency is there and that is why there is such a fear of stopping altogether. If people didn't feel dependent, then everybody would find it easy to stop drinking whenever they wanted but you and I know that even going on the wagon can be hell. Whereas experts say that if you are not in control, you have 'Dependency Syndrome,' I am stating categorically that the vast majority of drinkers are never in total control of their intake and therefore must have Alcohol Dependency Syndrome. It is not a choice for the drinker, it is necessity.

'EITHER THE DRINK GOES OR I GO.'

Some people will say this as a way of, hopefully, getting their partners to quit drinking. This rarely, if ever, works as the drinker will choose the drink over their partner. It's not because they choose to drink nor is it because they do not love their partner; it is because the decision is being made for them. Their judgement and rational thinking is always 'under the influence' of alcohol.

The first thing I need you to realise is that most people who regularly drink alcohol are not in control of their drinking. They are hooked. Just because they believe they are in full control, does not make it the case. It is never possible to be in real control of any drug as the drug will always control its victim, whether they realise it or not. The biggest advantage to stopping drinking is freeing yourself from the constant battle of trying to keep control (I will explain more later). It is this conditioning that has caused people to feel ashamed if they have had to seek help to quit alcohol. In fact, while you are reading this book you may be hiding the cover, or not telling people about your intentions. The irony is that they are probably drinkers caught in the same trap themselves.

There is such stigma attached to admitting you are hooked and this must be changed. On the whole people just don't realise they are addicted. In fact many drinkers have lived and died without ever realising it. For many years people had no idea they were hooked on cigarettes and it was only when smoking became antisocial and was banned in public places that smokers became aware of their addiction. They soon realised that they were not choosing to smoke but had to smoke. Most drinkers, however, are unaware of this. They believe that if they are managing to control their intake, they are in charge. However, what happened with prohibition, when all alcohol was banned? It resulted in organised crime because it soon became clear that people were not choosing to drink, they had to drink. Would the same thing have happened if they had banned bananas? The brainwashing, conditioning and illusions created by alcohol have caused people to believe they cannot live without it. I used to believe that I was actually choosing to drink and could stop whenever I wanted. I never really thought that I was hooked. But if that really was the case, why did I find it hard to stop for more than a week and why did the thought of stopping drinking for good fill me with fear?

The hard truth is that alcohol is a drug and one hell of an addictive one at that. Like any drug, its nature is to drag you further and further into its subtle life and soul-destroying clutches. However, contrary to the indoctrination by organisations like AA and despite the collective belief among drinkers that life just wouldn't be worth living without the most heavily advertised drug on the planet, there is some very good news for anyone caught in the alcohol trap ...

It's Easy to Stop Drinking

Not only is it easy to stop drinking, but the process of stopping is enjoyable and it is easy to stay off the stuff too. That is precisely what this book is all about; showing you just how easy it can be to stop drinking and stay off alcohol. This can be achieved without the need for willpower, discipline, misery or feelings of deprivation. The truth is that it has always been easy to stop drinking alcohol but we are conditioned to believe otherwise. The problem I had when I tried to quit was that I had approached it in the wrong way for so long that I was convinced that it was difficult to stop. Also, society has taught us that it is not only difficult but almost impossible to achieve true freedom from alcohol. This is another reason why people try to cut down or control their intake rather than stop altogether. After all, what is the point in trying to escape from prison when you have been conditioned to believe that there is no possible chance of freedom? The next best thing is to make prison life somehow more bearable.

Over the years I made several attempts to stop drinking. Well, when I say stop, I guess I mean cut down. The thought of actually quitting FOREVER put the fear of God into me. I often went on the wagon just to prove that I wasn't hooked and that I was in control but surely this just proved that I was. I once read a book called *How to Stop Drinking for a Month* in which the author stated that alcohol is the most wonderful thing on the planet, that you will definitely miss drinking and that you will find it very difficult to stop. However, he suggests you should stop for a month every now and then, just to prove that you are in control. In control? What is he talking about? You have just bought a book explaining how to give up alcohol for a month; surely that is proof in itself that you are not in control. If you were in control and could take it or leave it, you would simply stop. You certainly wouldn't need the help of a book would you?

A few years ago I would never have believed that, not only was it easy to stop drinking but that I would ever contemplate stopping forever, enjoy the process and never miss it again. However, that is exactly what happened and I now want to show the world exactly how we have all been fooled so that everyone else can find freedom, gain true control and achieve what is apparently impossible.

People who realise they are in the alcohol trap and want to get out are led to believe that they are somehow different to 'normal' drinkers and have lost control. Immediately they are branded with the title 'alcoholic.' We are taught that we are born with the disease alcoholism and can never really be free. So why should you be happy when you stop? In the poor drinker's mind there is nothing to be happy about. On the contrary, there is something to be very miserable about – the prospect of a lifetime of deprivation. So we are conditioned, not only by our own attempts to stop but also by society, into thinking that quitting alcohol and being completely free is impossible to achieve. We hear of people going to rehab clinics to dry out for months and still not being free, yet the beautiful truth is that it is easy to stop drinking and not to miss it for one reason alone – there is nothing to miss. It is all one huge lie that we have been conditioned to believe, not only by society but also by the clever illusions created by the drug itself.

Why is it difficult to stop drinking? This should be the real question. After all, you don't even need to do anything. All you have to do is not drink alcohol. If you were trying to navigate your way around the world in a hot air balloon, that would be difficult. If you had to run a hundred metres in under ten seconds, then it might take years to reach peak physical condition and, even then, you might not be physically capable of achieving it. So why do people, when they have reached the stage where they want to stop drinking, knowing that it is slowly destroying them both physically and mentally, find it so difficult to achieve? It is simply because, although they strongly believe that alcohol is destructive, they still think it provides some sort of genuine pleasure or crutch. They have reached a stage where they know the disadvantages outweigh the advantages but, despite that, still believe there are benefits to drinking alcohol. While the drinker continues to believe this, he or she will always find it very difficult to quit or feel miserable when they have. This is why it was so difficult for me during my three month experience on the wagon.

Once the illusions have been removed and the drinker realises that they were caught in an ingenious trap, then the penny finally drops and they realise that there are absolutely no advantages whatsoever to drinking alcohol. Then, and only then, is true freedom possible. If the illusions and years of brainwashing have not been removed fully and they continue to believe they have made a genuine sacrifice, then, even if they do not drink, they will still never feel truly free. As I said earlier, in order to escape from any trap you must realise you are in one but it is just as important to appreciate that you are free once you have escaped. Unfortunately the drinker is told he can never escape so he never feels free. In his mind he hasn't reached the stage where he is relieved not to need a drink. He is always in the process of stopping drinking as it continues to be a 'work in progress.'

Many years ago I saw ex-England footballer Paul Merson being interviewed on TV. Most of the interview was about his drinking, or not drinking to be more precise. Paul was undoubtedly to be admired for what he has achieved after announcing that he was an alcoholic. The problem was that at the time he didn't seem to know that he was free because he didn't feel free. Somebody gave him a label and told him that he can only ever expect a satisfactory way of life. They told him that he was going to have to battle the desire to drink for the rest of his life. In fact, in the interview he said that he was still taking one day at a time. No wonder we don't look forward to quitting. Paul struggled for over four years then fell off the wagon. During those four years he felt as though he couldn't go out and have fun like everyone else. He was told that he was different, so he felt different. He felt miserable and deprived about not being able to drink for four years. No wonder he eventually succumbed. I do not know whether Paul is drinking or not now but I can only hope that he has read this book, or found another way, and is now finally free. The alcohol trap is very simple and my only question is: 'Why did it take me so long to figure the whole thing out?' It is easy to stop drinking and enjoyable to be free for the rest of your life. All we need to do is remove the brainwashing and conditioning because that is the source of our addiction.

To be honest, some of the advice given by so-called alcohol addiction experts perpetuates the illusion that you will find it difficult, or even impossible, to stop drinking. They imply that you will have to go through months of torture and that it won't be easy. 'It's a long road ahead,' they might say. Well perhaps it is. If you go about it the wrong way but then so is Rubik's Cube until you discover the solution.

One of Drinkline's old pamphlets reads: *The Effective Strategies to Help you Cope with Stopping Drinking*. The words 'cope with' already imply that to stop drinking is difficult. They suggest, once again, that you can never be free but only come to terms with or 'cope with' stopping the drink. They then proceed to give you a list of 'effective strategies' to hinder you (oh sorry, I mean help you!). I have already mentioned one of these strategies that states you should:

Note down all the reasons why you want to stop

I have already explained why this strategy doesn't help people to stop drinking but in fact makes it harder to quit. Logically it should help, but everything about alcohol addiction that appears logical is in fact usually the complete opposite. When a drinker is stressed or under pressure, he will reach for a drink, so listing all the reasons why he shouldn't will simply remind him of what he already knows. That will usually make him even more stressed and pressurised than he was before he created that list. So what is the first thing an alcohol addict is likely to do? Have a drink to try and block his mind to what he already knew anyway of course. As I have said, people do not drink for the reasons they shouldn't, but for the reasons they want to drink, so this piece of advice clearly doesn't help people to stop, no matter how many experts say otherwise. Now let's explore some of the other 'helpful' strategies mentioned in this pamphlet.

Change your routine – perhaps choose different routes to the office or shops, avoiding pubs and off-licences

In other words, they are suggesting that you remove temptation. Again, this seems logical advice but it is in fact nonsense. They are telling you that you should somehow avoid the 200,000 pubs and off-licences in the UK on your way to the office or shops, avoiding those selling alcohol, otherwise you will be exposed to temptation. Presumably you shouldn't watch television or listen to the radio either as alcohol is often advertised there. The advertisements always present drink as pleasurable and marvellous, so you might be tempted if you watch or listen and, again, you would be failing to follow their strategy. You might as well never go out again, as you may be tempted to drink in the company of other drinkers. What about the likelihood that you have also had alcohol with a meal? Do you never eat again? Think about it, how can you avoid temptation if you still want to drink? When I drank every lunchtime, at every meal, every evening and every day, I was tempted. So, in order not to be tempted, you should never wake up. Even then, you might be dreaming about having a drink. The fact is that if you still want to drink, you will be tempted no matter where you walk to or from.

Discover different ways to relax

Different ways to relax? This is another huge part of the brainwashing (which we will destroy later on) implying that alcohol genuinely relaxes you. The beautiful truth is that you won't need to find different ways to relax as you will be far more relaxed as a non-drinker anyway. It is alcohol that causes you to feel un-relaxed in the first place as I will demonstrate later.

Take up old interests and activities you used to enjoy or explore new ones

What old interests do they mean? I started drinking when I was at school so I guess I should get out my skateboard instead of having a drink. This would prove very difficult to do while eating and this advice perpetuates the fear that you will no longer be able to the same things as a drinker, like socialising. You will soon realise that this is rubbish.

Try different types of soft drinks – you may like them!

Oh come on. If you don't have anything constructive to say, say nothing. Do they think we are children? In fact, would you dream of telling your child something so patently obvious? There I was, an alcohol addict for years, and all I had to do was drink soft drinks instead of alcoholic ones and my problem would be solved? Why didn't *I* think of that?

Do something while you drink at a social venue such as play darts, bingo or dance

Are they on a wind-up with this one? Play darts? Of course there is ample proof to show that playing darts helps people to stop or cut down on drinking. I mean you have only got to look at the bellies of some top darts players to see that!

Prepare yourself – rehearse saying 'NO' to offers of alcoholic drinks

Yes, you read correctly. In fact they go one stage further and ask you to stand in front of a mirror and rehearse saying 'No.' They even suggest ways that you could do it: 'No thanks, maybe next time.' 'No thanks, I'm driving.' 'Not now.' Can you imagine what an idiot you would feel doing that? They also suggest that you rehearse with a friend! Friend? You would have no friends left if you started doing that!

'Take each day at a time'

First of all it's a ridiculous suggestion anyway. 'Take each day as it comes'; how else can you live? Whether you drink or not, you have no choice but to take each day at a time. The main problem with this 'strategy' is that it gives the strong impression that the drinker will have to battle all day and every day, coping without drink one day at a time for the rest of his life. There are people who have been going to AA meetings for over twenty years and still stand up and say, 'I am Albert, I am an alcoholic.' How on earth can they be an alcoholic if they haven't had a drink for over twenty years? I have always thought an 'alcoholic' can be recognised as someone who drinks to excess on a regular basis, someone who drinks first thing in the morning or somebody who cannot cope without a drink. Paul Merson said during that interview that he was 'taking each day ... ' and that he was going to have to battle and suffer for the rest of his life. What a grim prospect. Suffer? Battle? With what? I suffered too but that was when I was drinking; not now. One of the greatest joys of being free is to no longer have to struggle to gain control, not to have to use willpower or discipline to limit my intake, or to suffer mentally and physically as a result of alcohol. One of the biggest mistakes people make when they stop drinking is to start counting the days. It's as though each day they are waiting to see whether they fail. It's no wonder they don't look forward to quitting as we are constantly conditioned to believe we can never be truly free; that we will always have to battle.

RUBBISH!

Drinkers really can get free and it's easy. The truth is that they already know that it's easy to stop drinking. If you think about it, they actually do that every time they finish a drink. The problem is not picking up the next one, and the one after that and the hundreds, if not thousands, after that.

> Drinkers really can get free and it's easy.

My main bone of contention with organisations like Drinkline and AA is that they suggest you are making a real sacrifice, that you will be missing out on some sort of genuine pleasure or crutch and that you will never be able to drink 'normally' again because you have a problem. In the Paul Merson interview, he was asked what he would do when the FA Cup was passed around filled with champagne. Paul said sheepishly, 'I would just pass it on and have a lemonade.' This question was odd for two reasons. First, why ask the question? It seems strange to ask somebody who you know doesn't drink alcohol what he would do with champagne. It would be like asking a vegetarian what they would do if offered meat. What did he expect him to do? I would imagine he would carry on celebrating on winning the most important trophy in English football. The question was inappropriate for another reason. The real question should have been, 'Do you think that you will win the FA Cup' or 'How would it feel to win the Cup?' Why does drink even enter into it? That part of his life is over (or so you would think). But it wasn't, because in his mind he was still not free. He was pining for something which he hoped he would never have again.

He had stopped drinking for over four years so there was no trace of the drug in his body, yet he and many like him still suffer after they stop. Some people haven't had a drink in years and are still dying for a drink and feeling miserable. They are still fighting the desire to drink. But where is the physical addiction? Open your mind and ask yourself this question. We have been told that the physical addiction is where the problem lies. But is it? When drinkers go into a clinic to 'dry out' for six weeks, they come out with no trace of alcohol in their system yet still have the desire to drink. Most people who go through the awful experience of drying out usually have a drink within the first week of leaving. When I stopped for those three months, the desire or craving for a drink got *worse*. If it was the physical addiction that caused the craving for the alcohol drug, then I would have been free after only a few days. Alcohol leaves the body very quickly which is essential as it is a powerful poison and if the body stored it we would die. In fact every trace of alcohol has gone after the first week to ten days. I will repeat this medical fact for those who have been conditioned to believe otherwise.

Every trace of alcohol has gone from the addict's system within seven to ten days after their last drink. So why anybody needs to dry out for six weeks is a complete mystery. You may already know that there are certain drugs, like disulphiram, which are prescribed to help keep people off alcohol. If you take disulphiram and drink just a tiny amount, it can make you very ill. The drug (apparently) should be continued until the craving for alcohol is lost.

Let me ask you a question: is there any sense whatsoever in taking one drug to get off another? If you think it works for heroin, think again. Methadone, the opioid drug used to wean addicts off heroin, kills more people than the heroin itself. It does not cure the addiction; it simply moves the problem without removing it.

It is ludicrous to think that this kind of approach would be effective in stopping people drinking. You are warned that if you take disulphiram and drink alcohol you may become acutely ill. Acutely ill? If you are hooked on alcohol and somebody says to you, 'Here, have this drug. After you take it you will not be allowed to drink alcohol. If you do it will make you feel ill.' What do you think you would do? You wouldn't stop drinking, you would stop taking disulphiram. Drinkers are not put off by becoming ill, acutely or otherwise. Most drinkers have suffered a humdinger of a hangover at least once. Does that stop them? As for the advice on continuing with the drug until the craving has gone, how long would they expect you to be on this drug? According to them the craving never goes, so the answer must be

– forever. The craving is not physical. The reality is that if you were to put a drug in your body which prevented you from drinking alcohol at all, then you would crave it even more as the craving is not physical, it's psychological. The problem is the way the drug is perceived in the addict's mind. I never suffered physically when I was on the wagon. I was suffering mentally because I felt deprived of something that I wanted. I was miserable in my mind, not my body. I was in a tantrum state, rather like a child who is not allowed to have his or her toy. I was suffering from mental deprivation and nothing more.

> The problem is the way the drug is perceived in the addict's mind.

I'm not saying that some alcohol addicts or people who drink heavily from morning till night don't experience a degree of withdrawal. In fact, for some, their sugar levels are so shot and their body so starved of nutrients that, yes, they do indeed suffer physically when the supply of this liquid drug is suddenly cut off. But even in the most severe cases the sugar levels and nutrients can easily be replaced with some delicious freshly extracted raw juice and super fruit smoothies. However, for the vast majority reading this book, there just isn't any withdrawal worth taking about. I mean, exactly what physical withdrawal are we talking about here? Where exactly will it hurt? What does it amount to really? A hangover? How long does that last? A headache for a couple of days? We have all had our fair share of those and we have all got over them too. The drinker who has reached the stage where he has lost his home, job and family, all for the precious nectar, will not have endured all that heartache because they are afraid of a hangover.

The fear for most drinkers is that they will not enjoy or cope with their lives in the same way without alcohol. The only thing that keeps people hooked is the illusion created by the drug itself and the years of conditioning and brainwashing. That is why I am so excited about sharing this information with you. It is what makes this approach to stopping so easy and enjoyable. Drinkers are only hooked on what they have been brainwashed to believe alcohol does for them. The chemical effect of alcohol creates the illusions which seem to confirm all this brainwashing. All we have to do is remove the brainwashing, then the addiction is automatically removed.

I am fully aware that if you have tried for years to break free and found it difficult, then accepting what I am saying at this stage may be hard. I am not asking you just to agree with everything I am saying. I want you to be sceptical and to question not only your own views on alcohol but, more importantly, what society has led you to believe. I am also fully aware that there will be a number of people reading this who have never really considered stopping and perhaps believe they are not hooked. It really doesn't matter which category you fall into as, providing you open your mind, this book will change forever the way you look and think about the drug called alcohol.

So if the addiction is over 90 per cent psychological and only about 10 per cent physical then, in order to break free, all we need to do is remove the brainwashing and make sure you have some live nutrients flowing through your system during the first week or so to help with any 'hangover' from the addiction. Information about live nutrients can be found on my website, www. juicemaster.com

We need to understand, not why people shouldn't drink alcohol because we are all fully aware of that, but the real question which is ...

Why Do People Drink Alcohol?

The answer is that we have been conditioned to drink alcohol from a very early age. Because of the illusion alcohol creates, people believe that there are genuine benefits to drinking and the sad reality is that it is so much a part of our identity as a nation. Somehow we have reached the stage where it is the only drug on the planet that, if you don't take it, people think you must either be suffering from a mythical disease known as alcoholism, are driving or are some kind of freak.

If you stop smoking you are a hero, if you come off heroin you are congratulated on your achievement but so strong is the alcohol indoctrination that, if you stop drinking, people think you need medical assistance for the rest of your life. Why?

It may be because around 80 per cent of the population is being conned by the same delusions and feel dependent on them. They know that just the thought of never drinking again instils such fear that they are convinced that stopping for good means suffering forever.

Alcohol really has everyone fooled. The brainwashing is so severe that it would be hard not to get hooked on alcohol because of the social pressure that exists to get you hooked in the first place. Almost from the moment we are born we are bombarded with information telling us that alcohol not only makes you an adult but portraying drinkers as heroes and heroines. The strong are made stronger and the weak are suddenly transformed into courageous and confident people because they drink. I don't suppose a single youngster, after seeing a tramp drinking lighter fuel first thing in the morning or watching somebody getting loud, argumentative, aggressive, abusive, nasty, violent, overemotional, obnoxious, stupid or slumped over the toilet vomiting, has ever been remotely tempted to try their first alcoholic drink. Why not? After all, this is the reality of alcohol but why should we be expected to relate to this side of it when we are constantly being bombarded with the other, glamorous images of drinking? These show young, strong, wealthy, successful and attractive people, from film and pop stars to successful businessmen and women, having a good time drinking. Doctors, lawyers, friends, family, partners, in fact everyone, it seems, is constantly telling us that drink equals a good time. We even have doctors telling us that alcohol is good for you, a point I shall cover later.

We have been conditioned to believe that any form of celebration must involve alcohol; otherwise it is just not a celebration. Christmas, New Year, birthdays and christenings ('let's wet the baby's head'), weddings, holidays, weekends, competition wins, new jobs, pay rises and engagements. Let's drink to this, let's drink to that; in fact, let's drink to anything just as long as we drink.

Every year, £200 million alone is spent on advertising alcohol in the UK. The government earns over £8.7

billion a year from alcohol and there's another contradiction. The last government earned this at the same time as they increased the drinking hours and condemned drinking. How perverse is that? As a nation we spend nearly £25 billion on alcohol per year, almost as much as the entire UK education budget of £27 billion which, in itself, represents 13 per cent of the total public expenditure for 2009.

It seems strange that society is often very judgemental when it comes to other forms of drug addiction; forms of drug addiction that they are fortunate enough not to be addicted to! Before I understood fully the nature of drug addiction I would often be the first in line to judge drug addicts. I wasn't a drug addict myself, after all I only smoked and drank alcohol; it wasn't as if I was on heroin or anything silly. It wasn't like I was on heavy drugs, or so I thought.

Society in general is always getting on its high horse about other forms of drug addiction. People often call for life sentences for heroin pushers or ecstasy dealers. I am not saying that this is wrong, nor am i condoning other drugs, but alcohol kills more people every year than heroin, crack, cocaine, speed, ecstasy, in fact all other hard drugs combined. Whereas 'hard' drugs kill about 1,000 people a year in the UK, alcohol kills over 9,000. Yes, you read correctly, over twenty-four people die each day of alcohol abuse in the UK alone and that is just the tip of the iceberg. There are also the alcohol *related* deaths which are estimated by the Royal College of Physicians to be around 40,000 a year and rising.

What is more, this costs the NHS £2.7 billion a year in treatment.

It is common to see people sitting with a cigarette in one hand and a drink in the other saying 'look at the youth of today on all these drugs' but do you know the name Leah Betts? You probably do. She is the poor girl who died of the drug ecstasy. Her picture was on huge billboards all over the country to highlight the dangers of that drug. Every TV station, radio programme and newspaper carried the story for months, some for years. There was an outcry calling for something to be done, to look at what the youth of today are on and to try the person who sold her the drug for murder. In which case, perhaps our government, along with the alcohol industry, should be tried for murder for the alcohol abuse and alcohol related deaths the drug has caused. After all, they are taking the biggest share of the profit from this legalised form of drug pushing aren't they? It is difficult to calculate the exact number of people killed by the effects of alcohol, particularly as many families ask doctors to leave out alcohol as the cause of death on the death certificate of a loved one.

There are so many people affected by alcohol in so many different ways. These include victims of sexual crime, physical and mental abuse, unwanted pregnancies, violence, family break-ups, the 75 per cent of stabbings directly attributable to alcohol, suicides, murders, rapes, beatings. There are between eight and fourteen million working days lost each year in the UK due to hangovers and alcohol is so often responsible for poverty and homelessness. I could fill a whole book with the death and destruction caused by alcohol and that is without the mental and physical abuse which alcohol inflicts on its victims. But that is not what this book is all about and, more importantly, it would not help the drinker to stop drinking. It might open their eyes a little more but they would still suffer from mental deprivation if they stopped. Drinkers already know these facts and, like all drug addicts, choose to block them from their minds.

The reason I mention these facts and figures is to illustrate once again that there is only one thing that keeps anybody addicted to alcohol and that is *fear*. There is the fear that we will not be able to enjoy or cope with our lives without a drink, the fear that we will have to go through some awful trauma in order to break free or, perhaps the worst fear of all, that we can never break free. But where did these fears come from? Who or what created them? Are they a part of our genetic make-up, character or personality? Are the fears there because we are weak willed? No, no, no. As I stated at the start of the book, it is the drug itself that creates the fear and all the brainwashing perpetuates and compounds it. As I will repeatedly emphasise, people are not so much hooked on the alcohol itself but what they have been brainwashed to believe it does for them. Think about it. The fears were not there before you started drinking were they?

Before you started drinking you could enjoy social gatherings without alcohol and you were perfectly happy. Now I am not saying that you were living a stress-free life before you started drinking. In fact, the most stressful period of many people's lives tends to be early childhood and adolescence. But when you were stressed as a child your first thought wasn't to fix yourself a drink to calm yourself down after a hard day at the nursery was it? When you went to jelly and ice cream parties you didn't need drink to enjoy yourself or to remove your inhibitions. In other words you were able to enjoy and cope with life without drinking alcohol. So why did you have that first drink? The answer is simple. It was because of all the pressure.

We end up believing all the nonsense about alcohol; all the advertising and brainwashing that makes you think you are not really an adult until you try your first drink. Our friends are doing it, our family does it, our film and TV heroes do it, so it is inevitable that we are going to have our first alcoholic drink. Unlike smoking or other drugs, we are not even told that alcohol is dangerous or addictive. Alcohol is the only drug known to kill over 160 people a week in the UK. We are even encouraged by our parents to drink alcohol. If you ask a smoker, 'Would you encourage your children to smoke?' the answer will be a clear, 'No way!' However, so strong is the brainwashing with alcohol that the same question to a drinker may result in a less clear-cut answer. Many parents give their children their first taste of alcohol before they have reached double figures. It is often a little glass of wine with a meal or a sip of beer from Dad's can. My grandmother even bought me a hipflask inscribed with my initials for my sixteenth birthday.

Alcohol is so much the 'norm' that it is a mystery how some people do not get hooked, not why they do. Is it any wonder that over 90 per cent of our male and 56 per cent of the female population drinks alcohol and even that is growing in the case of women?

Once we begin to realise that we are hooked on alcohol and that the physical addiction is easy to overcome, why do we find it so hard to quit? It's because we believe that we are making a genuine sacrifice and are actually 'giving up' something worth having. We feel mentally deprived when we stop. This feeling of deprivation is the real problem because even if you do not drink for years, but believe that you have 'given up' a genuine pleasure, then the feeling of deprivation and misery will last the rest of your life. That is why there are some people still going to AA for years after they have stopped drinking; miserable people still pining for a drink. That is why they are taking one day at a time. It is because they all feel as though they are missing out. They still feel deprived.

Who wants to go through life fighting a desire to drink or feeling miserable and deprived? The good news is that you won't have to. Once you understand fully why you drink and you begin to realise that alcohol does absolutely nothing for you then, for the first time in your life, you will start to realise that you will be giving up nothing and, for that reason, you will not feel deprived when you stop. You will not have to fight a desire; you will simply feel elated because you don't have to do it ever again.

SO WHAT DOES ALCOHOL GENUINELY DO FOR YOU ANYWAY – WHY DO PEOPLE DRINK?

It is possible to understand why we tried our first drink. It was because of all the indoctrination and pressure put on us, but what makes people have the second, third, fourth and hundreds of thousands of drinks after that? There are three main reasons why people drink alcohol. It's either for the pleasure (whatever the addict perceives that to be), because it's a crutch (stress reliever, relaxant, etc.) or because they believe that drinking has simply become a habit. There are a few drinkers who believe that the only reason they drink is because it has become a habit but I would like to lay this misconception to rest right now. People do not drink alcohol simply because ...

It's a Habit

I must admit that I used to believe I was drinking certain drinks simply out of habit. Not all of them of course; some were for pleasure and some to help cope with stress, but I honestly thought that some of my drinking was due to habit. But who was I kidding? Habit? The reasons we come up with to justify our drinking are amazing. Did I really think I left my house, went to the off-licence, came home, opened the bottle and drank it all out of habit? I do understand that we can all get into the routine of doing certain things, but it's easy to break other routines. For example, we drive on the left-hand side of the road in this country but when we go abroad, we switch to the right with no real problem. Some heroin addicts fool themselves into believing that they are injecting themselves through sheer habit as well. It's even referred to as a 'heroin habit' but anybody on the outside can see that it is pure drug addiction. If it were only habit they could just inject themselves with a syringe full of water. It would save them a fortune. If it were just a habit people could simply stop doing it.

Do you believe that people who lose their homes, family, self-respect, dignity, pride, self-worth and sometimes even their lives as a result of alcohol do so because they couldn't break a habit? Of course not; they do so because it's a drug addiction like any other. If you still think that some people are drinking out of habit, why is it that people who haven't had a drink in years are still taking one day at a time? Are they still in the habit of drinking alcohol? Are they still in the habit of buying alcohol? No, they are not. When you go on holiday to a place you have never been, to a hotel you have never seen and a beach you have never visited, are you in the habit of drinking on that beach at that time of the day? No. How long does it take to break this habit anyway? Is this the only habit in the world from which you are in permanent recovery? Is it the only habit that is never truly broken? Or is a more likely explanation that these people who haven't touched a drop in years and are still finding it hard to cope are simply feeling deprived because they still feel as though they are missing out on something pleasurable; that they are not like normal people but have a disease for which there is no known cure. The reality is that alcohol addiction is just that, an addiction and not a habit.

The problem with alcohol addiction is that most drinkers really have no idea that they are hooked. They honestly think they are drinking because they choose to and because they enjoy it. If they cannot think of a rational reason for why they are drinking they will resort to calling it a habit. We have told the same lies about alcohol for so long that we all end up believing them. I was constantly justifying why I drank, just as the majority of drinkers do. We instinctively know that we shouldn't be doing it and we instinctively know that it is not normal to poison ourselves. We sense that we are miserable at times if we are not allowed to drink. We even have moments when we sense we just might be hooked. So, in order to rationalise our drinking, we have to build up all these sound reasons for not being able to enjoy ourselves without first taking a drug. As you know, if you tell a lie for long enough and convincingly enough, even the person who started the lie will end up believing it.

The heroin addict may think they are getting high but any outsider can see clearly that they are simply trying to end the lows caused by the drug. All the over-sixteens who drink alcohol in the UK will also come up with rational reasons as to why they drink. If, collectively, they use the same reasons to justify their drinking, then we are bound to end up believing them, even if they make no rational sense whatsoever. Everything that I believed alcohol did for me was an illusion. The illusions simply confirm what we have heard for years, so we end up believing that alcohol provides a host of genuine benefits. But does it? One of the biggest delusions is that alcohol provides the drinker with a genuine pleasure. Exactly what pleasure is there in drinking alcohol? If it's a genuine pleasure then it can only come either from the taste, the thirst-quenching or the marvellous effect.

So let's remove the brainwashing a bit at a time. First of all let's get it clear that …

Taste Has Nothing to Do With It!

Taste really has nothing to do with why people drink alcohol. I understand that many people believe they love the taste of their favourite tipple but this is not why people drink. I used to believe that I loved the taste of a dry white wine, a pint of beer or a Southern Comfort but I now realise I never did. In order to remove this part of the brainwashing, let me ask you a question. How did your first alcoholic drink taste? Be honest. There isn't a single person in the world who, when they were having their first alcoholic drink, wasn't secretly thinking, 'What is this rubbish? I'd sooner have a fruit juice!' There isn't a person alive who, when they had their first drink, didn't feel physically and mentally sick. The reason is because alcohol is a poison.

The irony is that the awful taste is part of what springs the alcohol trap. Our fears of getting hooked are immediately removed because we are convinced that adults drink this muck because they actually enjoy the taste. Now, before you think I've lost the plot and there's nothing nicer on the taste front than a cool glass of white wine or an ice cold beer, hear me out. Have you ever drunk an alcoholic drink that you didn't like the taste of? No? Think about it. Of course you have. Everyone who drinks alcohol has on more than one occasion. When the pubs have closed and you go back to somebody's house for a nightcap and they only have a drink that you normally don't like, do you have a coffee? I have left my house at three in the morning looking for an all-night kebab house and paid £15 for a bottle of wine which tasted like sewer water. I have drunk spirits that, if you put a match to them, would light up an area the size of London and I didn't like the taste. When you are on holiday and can't get hold of your usual tipple, do you stop drinking? I have seen people having wine with dinner saying that the taste was too sharp or too bland. So why drink it?

People delude themselves into thinking that they drink alcohol just for the taste but do they? I love bananas but if there are no bananas at a social gathering I don't feel deprived or get upset. If, after eating bananas, I woke up the next day and I felt as though I had just been run over by a truck, I wouldn't carry on eating them just for the taste. If somebody offered me a banana which tasted unpleasant, I wouldn't carry on eating it just because it's a banana. People say that certain drinks have an 'acquired taste' but what does an acquired taste really mean? It means that you didn't like it in the first place. If you liked it you wouldn't have to acquire a taste for it. The reality is that you don't even acquire a taste for alcohol; you simply build up a tolerance to the drug and get over the foul taste in order to get the alcohol into your body with the least possible aggravation.

Smokers believe that they enjoy the taste of cigarettes yet they never eat them. This just proves that if you tell yourself something for long enough you will end up believing it. What is alcohol anyway? If we get down to reality, it's simply fruit or vegetables that have gone off. They have fermented, which means it's off. It is in the process of decay; it is rotten. That is why it tastes awful. Pure alcohol (or ethanol) is a colourless liquid and powerful poison. All poisons taste awful; they are meant to so we don't harm ourselves. 'Yes, but surely when mixed with other liquids, alcohol tastes good?' No, alcohol never tastes good. The whole object of the mixers is to try to cover up the foul taste. The first drinks that we tend to have are those that have been flavoured with fruit that hasn't gone off: Martini and lemonade, Pernod and blackcurrant, vodka and tomato juice and so many other cocktails. Then in 1995 there was the launch of the so-called 'alcopops' with drinks like Vodka Reef and Bacardi Breezer.

Alcopops have a higher alcohol content than normal strength beers and are one of the fastest growing alcoholic drinks sectors of all time: sales tripled during the first year. Is this really a surprise? Of course not. It's bound to be successful, as they don't taste like alcohol; they taste like orange, lemonade, blackcurrant or apple. All children love fruit and hate alcohol. So the alcohol industry dreamed up this plan to get even more people hooked on the stuff. 'The earlier we get them, the quicker we get them hooked and the more profit we make. Hooray!' I know, let's cover up the foul taste of the poison alcohol with fruit flavours that the young naturally like and give the drinks names that are cool like Two Dogs (whose slogan 'It's the dog's ... ' of course means 'it's the dog's bollocks,' urban slang for 'the best'). What rebel teenager could refuse?

A report from Alcohol Concern states: 'An established control on young people's drinking has shown that youngsters find traditional alcoholic drinks unpalatable. With alcoholic lemonade, cola, flavoured milk, etc., this control has been removed.'

I remember sitting down to Sunday dinner when I was eleven and being allowed to have a small glass of wine with the meal. How grown up I felt; what a psychological boost for a young man. I would sip it very slowly and literally shudder after every mouthful. I hated the taste of it yet, later on in life, I could at times get through three bottles in a night. What had changed? Had the taste changed? No, the difference was that I was addicted and couldn't enjoy myself without it. I was justifying my intake by saying that I enjoyed the taste. I had said it for so long that I really believed it.

There is so much brainwashing involved even with the taste of alcohol. On the one hand you have your rational brain that knows your first alcoholic drink tasted revolting and on the other, wine connoisseurs telling us that the taste of certain wines are worth hundreds, sometimes thousands, of pounds. Do you honestly believe that any bottle of wine is worth thousands of pounds? You may well think at this stage that I'm just an uncultured git, unable to tell the difference between fine wine and sewer water. But in my mind there is no such thing as a 'fine wine' any more than there is 'fine heroin.' It is just the way it is advertised. Why is the person who drinks beer perceived differently to the person who spends thousands of pounds on a 'superior' wine? It's for one reason and one reason alone: the brainwashing and conditioning. The person on a park bench drinking their alcohol from a can and getting their nicotine from a roll-up is seen very differently to the person smoking a hundred pound cigar and drinking the 'finest' champagne. But why is that? They are both taking the same drugs aren't they? What is the difference between caviar and taramasalata? They are both fish eggs. It is the conditioning that creates the belief, that's all. This is an area I don't fully expect you to agree with me on and I am more than aware that some readers may wish to close the book at this stage. You may think I am saying there is no difference between Blue Nun wine and Cristal Champagne, when of course there is. However, please keep an open mind to the fact that conditioning has played a part at least in how you perceive the taste of your favorite tipple and that there is an enormous amount of brainwashing and snobbery when it comes to alcohol.

No more so I guess than the nonsense that comes out of the mouths of some 'wine experts' when describing it. Wines are described as flippant, cheeky, having a 'good nose,' precocious, sombre and even mysterious. The only mystery is why we fall for the hype in the first place. Next time you see one of these 'experts' with their nose deep in a large glass, just ask yourself if you feel they should have the vote. Especially when you see them spitting it into a bucket after they have tried it! We don't question what we have seen for years, but seriously it's crackers.

Have you ever sent back a bottle of wine at dinner? Very few people have, even if they are unsure as to the taste of that wine and think it a bit sharp or even that it might be a little 'corked'; they still nod and say yes. I know I have, many times. After all, we don't want to look uncultured or lacking in sophistication. What is all this nonsense anyway? It's because it is part of the pretentious rubbish that keeps people hooked. As I've mentioned before, if you say something for long enough you can end up believing it. It all tastes like rubbish, because it is rubbish, literally.

If you persevere with any drink that contains alcohol, you will eventually get used to the foul taste and you will end up liking it. This creates the illusion that you actually enjoy it. The taste doesn't change just because you persist with it but remains identical to the very first fix you had. Your brain and body have simply built up an immunity and tolerance. If you still think that taste has got something to do with why you drink alcohol, why not drink non-alcoholic drinks? There are some on the market that taste exactly the same as 'normal' alcoholic drinks but that just wouldn't be the same would it? I tried drinking non-alcoholic beers and wines on many occasions but just couldn't get used to them, let alone want them. The reason for this was that there was no alcohol in them. Heroin addicts could inject themselves with a saline solution but that wouldn't be the same either. Reason? No heroin.

> If you persevere with any drink that contains alcohol, you will eventually get used to the foul taste and you will end up liking it.

If taste had anything to do with it, nobody would ever take their second alcoholic drink. Whether they admit it or not, most drinkers instinctively feel stupid drinking – after all, when you think about it, it is a bit odd standing around with a drink that makes you steadily less in control of your faculties. However, they can block this from their minds most of the time as the majority of people are doing the same thing. If you are doing something collectively, which goes against rational judgement, you do not have to come up with any reasons to justify your actions. It is only when you are alone that you really start questioning it. Nobody likes to take any drug alone. I do not mean with nobody else around; I mean as a lone drinker in the company of people who are not drinking. This is one of the only times when people really question their drinking. This is when we instinctively start to know that what we are doing is stupid.

For years smoking was also viewed in the same way. At one time it was even unusual not to smoke. Smoking was never seen as drug addiction and many people had no idea they were hooked; that is until now. They only realised they were hooked when they had to stand outside buildings in the freezing cold to get their fix. Smokers also say they like the taste of certain brands of cigarettes but if they cannot get hold of their usual choice, they will smoke any make simply to get the nicotine into their system. I deluded myself for years that I loved the taste of alcohol. Yet if my usual tipple wasn't available, I would drink anything that contained alcohol, even if it tasted disgusting.

Poisons in themselves can never taste good, they were never meant to. Alcohol however is a liquid and should, in theory, quench your thirst. Quenching your thirst is a genuine pleasure as I'm sure you'll agree but, again, this is one of the many misconceptions surrounding alcohol. Let me prove to you why alcohol is incapable of ...

Quenching Your Thirst

Here is one of the cleverest parts of this whole confidence trick. Alcohol is a diuretic, which means that it makes you pee. Have you ever noticed how you drink one beer but pee out three? This process dehydrates the body. You may know this already as you have probably experienced the 'Sahara Desert' syndrome when you wake up during the night and find yourself trying to pour fifty gallons of water down your throat in a minute flat. You also notice that a man has moved into your head and is mercilessly pounding the inside of your skull. This is because your brain has shrunk. Yes, you read correctly, your brain is now smaller than it was the day before because the brain is mainly made up of water as, indeed, is the rest of the body. The more alcohol you take in, the more water you lose. It's a simple mathematical equation. What you are feeling is the pounding effect of blood trying to pump through your dehydrated brain.

With water you only need one or two glasses to quench your thirst but because alcohol causes dehydration I managed to get through as many as sixteen pints of lager at one sitting. The more I drank, the more dehydrated I became. The more dehydrated, the thirstier I was. The thirstier I was, the more beer I would drink. It was a vicious circle. Even bearing in mind that the alcohol content of the whole drink is usually very low and the rest of the drink is made up mainly of water, this additional water is still insufficient to mitigate the diuretic quality of alcohol. Alcohol dehydrates so much that even with as little as 3 per cent alcohol and 97 per cent water, the 3 per cent will not only use up the 97 per cent but also rob the body of its own stores.

I'm not saying for a second that a pint of beer after a game of football or rugby, or a glass of wine at lunchtime on a hot sunny day doesn't quench your thirst at all, but the alcohol in the beer or wine certainly didn't do it. You wouldn't drink neat alcohol to quench your thirst would you? Alcohol itself is incapable of quenching thirst; it actually makes you thirsty. What a product! The people who make and sell alcohol are on to a real winner. They are selling a liquid which makes you thirsty, so you buy more to try to quench the thirst which it created in the first place. Very clever!

This is a subtle part of the pleasure trap and I will soon explain how alcohol is incapable of providing genuine pleasure. However, when you have an aggravation, like thirst or a headache for example, then ending that aggravation is pleasurable. But would you deliberately cause yourself the aggravation to make it pleasurable when it is relieved? Again, the drug is creating a low but deceives its victims that the ending of that low is a genuine pleasure. I could not drink sixteen pints of water in one evening. That is because water is genuinely capable of quenching thirst but alcohol does the complete opposite. So part of the illusion of enjoyment is momentarily ending the thirst aggravation created by that previous drink. In the end, you would eventually need some water hence the 'Sahara Desert' syndrome which is the body's cry for help.

So if it's not for the taste, and it's not to quench your thirst, then it must be for the ...

Marvellous and Pleasurable Effect

Ah yes, the marvellous and pleasurable effects of alcohol; that rather strange feeling in the brain caused by alcohol. But what is that strange feeling? Is it a genuine pleasure and does it really make us feel truly happy? Can we ever really explain or describe 'that' feeling anyway?

When you are doing something you instinctively know to be stupid, you come up with any reason to justify what you are doing, not only to other people but also to yourself. If you say it for long enough, you end up believing it and will not question whether or not what you are saying makes any rational sense.

Heroin addicts believe they enjoy injecting themselves with a powerful poison which will zombify and stupefy them. They believe that the destruction of their lives is the price they have to pay in order to get 'that' marvellous pleasure. Alcohol addicts also believe they enjoy drinking a poison that will zombify and stupefy them. They just don't get that the destruction of their lives is the price they have to pay in order to get 'that' marvellous pleasure. But, when it comes to alcohol, the biggest illusion is that it can genuinely make us feel happier.

I have said that I loved drinking. I honestly thought I did at the time but now I see clearly that I had simply fallen for a very clever trick. Alcohol fools you into thinking that you are getting true pleasure when you are not. Heroin addicts think they get genuine pleasure when they stick that needle into their arm and fill their vein with heroin but all they are actually enjoying is the relief from the awful lows that the drug itself has created. The poor heroin addict is in a constant fight to stay out of that depression and desperate to get back to the state they were in before they started taking the drug. In fact the only reason they continue to take heroin is to try to feel like a person who doesn't need to take heroin.

The only problem is that they are trying to gain control over something that is in fact controlling them. The more they try, the more they lose it and the more they lose it, the harder they try to regain it. The body will always build up an immunity and tolerance to any drug; it's the survival mechanism. So the more of the drug they take, the less relief it provides and the less it relieves them, the more they need.

Many heroin addicts will often go back to the drug even after they have gone through withdrawal. Some stop for years but are still taking one day at a time. They say they are never really free as they could go back at any time but, for today, they are resisting it. The sad truth is that they are pining for a pleasure that does not exist. They continue to feel mentally deprived because they believe they 'gave up' a pleasure.

Alcohol works in exactly the same way. This is why there are many people in the world who have stopped drinking but still feel there is a void. They take one day at a time trying to resist the marvellous pleasures of alcohol according to the AA philosophy. Unfortunately these people are also pining for something that does not exist. They are going through mental deprivation for nothing. While they still believe they have made a sacrifice, they will always feel the void to some degree, confirming their belief that alcohol fills that emptiness. But it is how they think that actually created the void and the feeling of inadequacy in the first place.

When you stop, you actually return to normal. We never needed alcohol before we started drinking; the need arose afterwards. I remember going to parties as a child and I did not need alcohol to enjoy myself. I never feared that Christmas or my birthday would be a disaster without alcohol. I never thought that one day I would reach the stage where I would panic at the thought of not being able to drink alcohol on my birthday; that the very thought of celebrating New Year without alcohol would scare the life out of me; that just contemplating the idea of going out at the weekend without drinking would make me miserable. I never thought I would become so lethargic and tired that my main source of pleasure would come from a bottle. I never thought that I would ever become dependent on a drug; that I would reach the stage where my confidence would be so shattered that I wouldn't be able talk to my friends without having a drink. When I was a child I never thought I would end up like the adults I saw.

If you were at a children's birthday party do you honestly think that they would be happier if they had some alcohol inside them? If you saw a child crying would you give them a drink to cheer them up? If you saw a child laughing would you give them a drink so that they could get even happier? Do you think that by giving a hyperactive child alcohol they would become relaxed? Of course you wouldn't because you would know for certain that alcohol would not relax them or make them happy; it would simply stupefy them. Would they enjoy that stupefied state? How could they? It would no longer be them. They would not be feeling any genuine feelings any more as alcohol numbs all the senses. The magnificent machine that is the human body would now be malfunctioning. When alcohol hits the brain it deprives us of our natural senses, leaving us unprotected and vulnerable. If you gave a child alcohol on their birthday, not only would they not get any genuine enjoyment but they would also miss that birthday. The alcohol would deprive them of that experience forever. How can you truly experience any emotion when you do not have access to your genuine feelings?

Children do not need alcohol to enjoy themselves so why do we feel the need? Why do we feel as though our lives would no longer be complete without alcohol? Why do we feel that something would be missing if we stopped drinking? It is because of the alcohol itself that we have these feelings. The alcohol creates our fears. We were complete before we started taking alcohol; it is only the drug itself that gave us the feeling of inadequacy. This means that drinkers experience a constant void and they try to fill that void with the very thing that created it in the first place. While they continue to believe they are not complete without alcohol, they will never feel truly complete, even if they stop.

Alcohol is a depressant that appears to cheer people up but only to the person 'under the influence,' not to a sober person. It is only the perception of the person drinking alcohol that has been changed, not those they come in contact with. I know that when I was sober and tried talking to someone who was drunk, the last thing I wanted was to feel the way they did. I could see they were not really happy. They were in a stupefied state. I could not communicate with them and it was not even worth talking to them because I could see clearly that it was not the real person. I was fooled into believing that this is what drink did but was convinced it never did that to me. After all, I felt better when I had a drink, or so I thought. Once alcohol enters the brain your perception changes. You feel a false sense of pleasure and of being in control. You actually believe you are happier. If you are with other addicts it appears normal as everybody is experiencing the same feeling, but what is this feeling anyway and do we ever really enjoy it? What true pleasure do we get from an alcoholic drink? If we had to sell it could we do it?

I remember my first experience of getting drunk. I was about ten years old and I drank some wine. The feeling was awful. The room was spinning, I felt sick and vomited. I felt completely out of control. The next day

I felt as though I had been run over by a steamroller. I never enjoyed it for one second. So, did the feeling change as I got older? No, the drug isn't different, just my perception, along with the many lies I concocted to deceive myself. The only difference was that my body had built up an immunity to and tolerance of the drug, so it took a lot more alcohol for me to reach that state. The first few drinks at lunchtime were just topping up the low feeling I went through in the morning, created by the drinks I had consumed the night before. As you will no doubt be aware, when you first start drinking one drink floors you, but gradually you manage more and more. Now it takes even more to do that. The alcohol itself hasn't changed, only your body's tolerance to the poison. Some people build up such a tolerance that, even while they are drinking, they still feel the need for a drink as the more they drink the greater the need and the greater the need, the more they drink.

Most drinkers are not aware of the fact that it can take 72 to 240 hours for your body to get over the physical effects of alcohol. That is up to ten days to recover from the low caused by the drug. Some people describe this as withdrawal. Most of the time this is imperceptible to the addict as they are used to feeling this low and regard it as normal. If they have more than their tolerance level, they will become more aware of the low that causes a hangover. Their body then builds up even more of a tolerance to the drug which happens every time they exceed their usual tolerance level. After a while they believe that the ending of the low is a true high which is about the same as putting on a pair of tight ski boots, wearing them for a couple of days, just so that you can get the pleasure of taking them off again.

Alcohol is a double-edged sword when it comes to creating the illusion. One is the partial ending of the physical low; the other is that it's mind altering. Drinkers believe that this is where the pleasure really lies, but does it? We say that we drink to get 'that' feeling but what is that feeling?

The feeling I thought I was enjoying is a short circuit in the brain – literally. People sometimes describe it as a feeling of being 'light headed' and say they enjoy the sensation. But isn't that the same as feeling dizzy? Well spin around then, it will save you a fortune – but if you do try spinning and then walking straight, you will fall over which is worth remembering. I never drank alcohol to make me feel dizzy; I drank it for the same reasons that heroin addicts inject themselves. It was because I felt as though I could not enjoy myself or cope without my drug. I never consciously thought this as I believed that I was getting a genuine pleasure from alcohol and that I was choosing to drink. In fact I was never choosing to drink and I was certainly never getting genuine pleasure from drinking.

Some argue that people laugh more when they're on alcohol. In some cases this is true, but when I was seven years old and living in Halifax, I used to hang around with a bunch of similar aged kids who always had smiles on their faces from sniffing glue. Is this a good reason to sniff glue? Is it genuine happiness they are feeling? Do their inane expressions mean that glue sniffers are genuinely happier than those who don't sniff glue? Of course not! However, the fact is that if you do drink alcohol ...

You Are Never Really You

Alcohol removes your natural fears and you become unprotected and vulnerable. The part that controls our rational and intellectual thinking disappears and we become literally stupefied when alcohol takes effect – a state also known as inebriation.

It is good to let your hair down once in a while and be a bit silly, I hear you cry. I agree and I do it frequently. You do not need alcohol for that; just look at children. At least when they do it, it is actually them so they can get the genuine pleasure of letting their hair down and fooling around. It would be fine if we could honestly enjoy that stupefied state but I believe that the biggest downside to being addicted to alcohol is that you are never really yourself. If you are taking the drug, you are not the real you; there is a part missing; you are incomplete. If you are not allowed to have some alcohol, you feel uptight and miserable so you are still not the real you. Alcohol takes away your natural senses so any feeling you have when under the influence is false. If we step outside the trap for a second and take a real look at the situation, we can see clearly that alcohol does not make people genuinely happy and that there is no real pleasure to be had from drinking alcohol.

Alcohol is a depressant. The longer you take a depressant the more depressed you become. This is an undisputed medical fact. If alcohol made people happy, then doctors would prescribe it as an anti-depressant on the NHS. If alcohol made people genuinely happy then, whenever they were really down and lonely, they could just sit indoors, drink a couple of bottles of wine or, better still, a bottle of scotch, and be as happy as pie again. The truth is, if you did that you would be even more depressed. If you are still in doubt then ask yourself why over 65 per cent of suicide attempts are alcohol related. If alcohol made you happy and merry why would you want to end it all? Surely when you are happy the last thing you would want to do is commit suicide?

Am I suggesting that I have never been happy while having a drink? No, of course not. Sometimes I was bound to be happy when I was drinking; it's the law of averages. I was happy not because of the drink but in spite of it. Really open your mind on this one and you will realise that it is never the drink that is making you happy as the alcohol never changes; it is only the occasions when you drink it and the people you are with.

When people go to funerals it doesn't matter how much they drink, they still feel sad. This is because it is a sad occasion. When people are at an exciting party with fun friends, they will be happy. This is because it is a happy occasion. At least, they should be happy but the sad truth was that if I was at a party and couldn't drink for whatever reason, I would be miserable. It wasn't that I was happy with alcohol but miserable if I couldn't have it. I would say, 'Parties are just not the same when you are not drinking' but I only felt this way because I was like a child having a mini tantrum; I felt as though I was missing out. I also felt almost naked without a drink in my hand and that I could not enjoy myself in the same way without my drinking partner – alcohol. Yet the alcohol never provided any genuine pleasure or enjoyment and it certainly never made a party although I was convinced that it did.

A party is always better when everybody has had a few drinks, isn't it? Well, answer this question if you will. Have you ever been to a really lousy party? Have you ever been to one of those dos that were boring as hell with dull and miserable people? If you haven't, I'd be very surprised. Let me ask you another question. Was there alcohol at this party? The answer is, of course, yes. I went to plenty of terrible parties and still do. Equally, you will probably have been to parties where you have been drinking and had a great time. So it's obvious that it's not the alcohol that determines whether you have a good evening but the company, the banter and the social aspect of being out with friends combined with the music and the dancing, but never the alcohol.

I used to say that I could easily enjoy myself without alcohol and, to justify my drinking, would come up with at least two occasions when I did not drink and was OK. It was to show others and prove to myself that it was not out of dependency but choice.

Answer this question. Each time you have had a drink, can you honestly say you have been happy? Have you ever been uptight or argumentative when drinking?

Have you ever been stressed out, felt depressed or cried during a drinking session? Have you ever become obnoxious or unreasonable when drinking? Think about it. If you have experienced any of these emotions while drinking, then it should be blatantly obvious that alcohol does not make you happy. In theory, every time you drink alcohol you should be laughing and enjoying yourself but you can't say that happens every time you drink, can you? If alcohol genuinely made you merry, wouldn't you agree that it should work every time you drink the stuff?

I bought into the idea that I could drown my sorrows in alcohol; after all, alcohol makes people happy doesn't it? So when you are feeling down, it should perk you up. The reality is the opposite; if you drink while you feel depressed, you will feel even more depressed than you were to start with. Do people look happy when they are smashing bottles into people's faces after drinking? 'But Jason,' you might say, 'this is what can happen if you have too much but a little alcohol does make you cheerful.' Hang on! Take too much alcohol and these things can happen but having a little makes you happy and merry? Who are we kidding? If alcohol makes you happy then surely the more you have, the happier you should feel, not the opposite? What is this 'a little alcohol is OK' business anyway? It is a drug and, as such, you are compelled to have more. Once you start drinking you have no real choice. You either continue drinking more and more, or you will have to exercise a degree of willpower, discipline and control in order not to increase your intake.

Recently someone asked me whether I had stopped drinking because I couldn't control my intake. I told them I had stopped because I did not want to control my intake any longer. It is a constant battle when you have to use willpower and discipline to try to stay in control. As I mentioned, it is the exercising of this control which means that you are not in fact in control. It is so nice to be free.

The only reason why a little alcohol appears to create happiness is because it removes natural fears and satisfies your psychological dependency on the drug. The truth is, you should be happy at social gatherings anyway. In the following chapters I will explain why the removal of your natural fears (caused by this short circuit in the brain) creates all of these illusions. However, the fact is that at the moment you are in a situation where you cannot be happy without alcohol on these occasions. You can continue telling yourself and anyone who will listen that you enjoy a drink but can you take it or leave it? Are you really in control of your drinking or is the alcohol, either consciously or subconsciously, controlling you? I will tell you now that every single person who drinks alcohol regularly is not in control. Alcohol addicts are dependent. Most think they aren't and believe they drink out of choice. The choice was never really ours to begin with so how do we know that it is our choice to continue to drink? It's not always easy to know so let's help clear up the confusion with this simple question that I have put to many drinkers, some with very little money and self-worth:

'If I said to you that you could have a lottery win of £100,000, would you take it?'

Of course everybody answers 'yes.' However, in order to keep the money there is just one tiny condition – you can never, ever drink alcohol again. What would you say? Would you have to think before making your decision? What decision would you make if you were honest with yourself? Would you take the money? I know what I would have said when I was hooked … stuff the money! What would be the point of all that money if you couldn't enjoy yourself and never have a drink again, even to celebrate? Think of the holidays you could have with all that money but what would be the point if you couldn't have a drink by the pool? Sod the money, let's have a drink!

That is the same answer I get from almost every drinker I have asked. At first, many said that they would take the money. I thought, 'Surely not, if you're honest.' Then I realised that most of them were not being honest. That is, after all, the nature of drug addiction; it makes you try to prove you are not dependent and are in control. All drug addicts lie, including drinkers, not only to other people but also to themselves. When I really pressed them and asked, 'Would it really not bother you that you could never drink ever again?' They said, 'Well if I am honest, not only would it bother me but, you are right, I wouldn't do it. There is more to life than money.' There is also more to life than alcohol but the addict does not see it that way.

The reality is not that alcohol makes you happy; it's that you are miserable without it. If you have drunk alcohol at every social occasion for years, you simply cannot imagine life without it. Your only reference to alcohol-free social gatherings is when you are forced not to drink because you are driving, on medication, being nagged, on the wagon or for some other reason. Your brain now tells you that a night without alcohol makes you unhappy and a night with alcohol makes you happy. But it's not the alcohol making you happy, it's just that you feel deprived when you can't have it, so you are miserable. This is because you have always relied on alcohol to help you enjoy a social gathering.

In the following chapters I will illustrate just how alcohol destroys your courage. Before you started drinking you relied on yourself and you were more than happy to do that. As I have explained, before you started drinking you could enjoy the highs without alcohol and handle the lows without the drug. Of course we had the usual fears, inhibitions, apprehensions and immaturity which all children experience but we quickly overcame them as we grew up. If you do not remember, look at children's parties. The children walk in with the usual apprehension but within five minutes they have destroyed the place. They do not need alcohol, heroin, crack, cocaine or any other drug; they are already on a high, a natural high, feeling great just to be alive. However, the addict will never achieve this as the drug caused them to feel incomplete in the first place. The irony is that they could so easily be in the same position if they did not drink alcohol but they can't as it is causing the very problem they are trying to solve.

What is this marvellous and pleasurable effect we think we get from drinking anyway? Is it the pleasure of not being able to communicate properly? Is it the marvellous effect of losing all your senses so that you become immediately vulnerable and completely unprotected from danger? Is it the wonderful feeling of becoming totally stupefied? Is it the great effect of not being able to focus or walk properly? Is it the pleasurable effect of talking complete and utter rubbish for hours on end? Is it the wonderful sensation of vomiting? Is it the pleasure of blowing your mind so much that you become a completely different person? Is it the marvellous effect of destroying your memory so you don't even recall your apparently wonderful experience anyway? Is it the marvellous and pleasurable effect of losing all the checkpoints between your brain and mouth so you get loud, aggressive, obnoxious, vulgar, nasty, hurtful, uptight, annoying, repetitive, pathetic, overemotional or abusive? Is it the marvellous effect of being out of control? Is it the wonderful effect of not being able to make love or show true love and affection because you are too 'out of it'? Is it the pleasure of saying and doing things that you will regret for many years to come? Is it the great sensation of dizziness? Just tell me, where and what is this marvellous effect? To be honest, I don't think you can as it just doesn't exist. It's one huge fallacy.

When you see people who are drunk and you haven't had a drink yourself, does it really make you want to have some alcohol so that you can get the same 'enjoyable' effect? For example when you see someone drinking from a can of beer in the middle of the street during the day, do you envy them? Not many drinkers do, but why not? Don't you want to have fun too? The fact is that alcohol can never make an evening or improve a holiday; it has certainly destroyed a few. However, alcohol gets the credit when, in fact, the good time has nothing at all to do with the alcohol.

I went to Tunisia a few years ago, when I was still drinking. The first few nights were spent in the hotel bar where they had some really 'stunning' acts for our entertainment. Personally I think a better time would have been had watching paint dry! Still, we were in the middle of nowhere and there didn't seem to be anywhere else to go. I was, of course, drinking every night. This makes me sound like a heavy drinker but every alcohol addict drinks virtually every night on holiday. This is because they have no restrictions preventing them from taking their drug and they feel as though they cannot enjoy themselves without it. The point is that, although I was drinking, the evenings were very, very boring and, if there is nothing to stimulate your mind when you are drinking, you get tired very quickly.

I was only there for a week and on the fifth day we decided to go on one of those pre-arranged evenings with a meal, entertainment and free wine all night. At the time, it was the last part that appealed. The evening was excellent; the best of the whole week and it made the holiday so much better. Was the evening so good because I was drinking? No, I had been drinking every night before that evening. It was because the atmosphere was excellent. There was belly dancing, snake charming, a room filled with about 500 people all clapping and dancing on the tables and the stage. I was dancing and interacting with others and it was really fun. I had an excellent evening, not because I was drinking alcohol but in spite of the fact that I was drinking. If someone had said to me at the time that there wouldn't be any drink, the sad truth is that I would rather have stayed in the hotel bar than attend the event. At the time I was convinced that some of the success of the night was due to the amount I drank but, looking back, I didn't actually drink that much as I was too busy dancing and having fun.

In fact, when I was hooked, there were several occasions when I had an excellent evening with hardly any drink. Haven't you ever been to a social gathering where you danced all night with very little to drink and realised at the end of the evening that you had a great time, yet hardly touched a drop? To your surprise you knew you could even have driven home. But if you had been told you couldn't drink, you would have felt miserable and deprived. The truth is that we do not need alcohol to enjoy ourselves, because alcohol does not make you enjoy yourself; it is a depressant. It also gives you the feeling that you are in control but in fact you are ...

Under the Influence

The biggest danger of the alcohol trap is that it gives the addict the illusion of control. This sounds like a contradiction, especially when you see someone who has drunk alcohol when you haven't, but alcohol removes one's natural fears and inhibitions. When that happens you feel as though you are more in control but, in fact, you are not. Consequently this leaves the drinker out of control, vulnerable and unprotected. When you are driving your car, you have to be alert in order to make sure you don't injure yourself or other people. It is natural to have some fear at these times as it's this fear which is vital for our survival. However, when alcohol short-circuits the brain, it removes this fear and gives the addict the illusion that they are calmer and more in control so their perception has now changed.

There are still some people who believe that they are better drivers when they have had a couple of drinks and I used to be one of them. Was I stupid for thinking this? No, the reality is that I did feel calm, more relaxed and in control at the time but these were illusions, and how was I to know when I was the one who was under the influence? When I woke up the next morning, my perception of what had happened had not changed. I felt hungover and thought I had been outrageously stupid to drink and drive but I still believed that the feelings I had experienced while under the influence were real.

They say that a good friend should never let you drink and drive. That is true and a good friend wouldn't. A friend who actually knows what they are doing that is. It is no good asking them to hang on to your keys so that you don't drive home if you have too much to drink. Once they are under the influence themselves, their judgement vanishes and it is not them any more. Your true friend has already left and the person who remains just wants to get home and wants you to provide the transport. You may drive to a pub with the best intentions in the world but, as soon as that alcohol hits your brain cells, you feel a false sense of control. You would never normally contemplate drinking and driving but it's no longer the real you who is driving home. 'Under the influence' means literally that: being controlled in what you say, do, and think.

Most people realise that alcohol drinkers do not drive better but are in fact endangering the lives of others as alcohol slows down their reactions. This awareness was highlighted partly due to the organisation MADD (Mothers Against Drunk Driving). Their campaign in the early eighties led to people changing their attitude to drink-driving but it still wasn't enough to make me ask myself whether all my other reasons for drinking were fallacies too. Take the idea that it makes you a fun person. Alcohol does not turn you into a fun person. How many people do you know who are dull and annoying and who, after a drink, don't turn into fun people? Far from it, they become even more boring and annoying and all you want to do is get rid of them.

In truth, alcohol does none of the things which we are convinced it does including the one about …

It Helps Me to Relax

In what situation does alcohol help us to relax? I used to find the drinks that helped me were consumed when I was in what should have been relaxing, situations anyway. We must keep this point very clear: the alcohol never changes. Circumstances change, situations are different; never the alcohol.

I would come home from work, fix myself a drink, put my feet up and think 'Aaah that's relaxing', but coming home from work and putting your feet up is relaxing anyway. It is a way to unwind from the pressures of the day. Most of the time I would take just one mouthful and think that it was the drink that was helping me unwind. It didn't even occur to me that the alcohol hadn't had time to take effect. The truth is that your brain will do as you tell it. If you tell your brain that you cannot relax without a drink then the brain will say 'OK, I won't relax until you get one then.' That explains why I could relax after just one sip but it was not the drink that helped me relax; it was just the relaxing situation.

In reality, the only reason for being my being so tense was partly due to my alcohol addiction. Alcohol does create withdrawal. However, unlike heroin where the withdrawal is very noticeable, alcohol withdrawal is very subtle. Now anybody who has reached the delirium tremens stage no doubt disagrees. What about the terrible physical withdrawal that is the DTs? Do we mean the shakes? Are we talking about not being able to hold a cup properly because our hands are shaking too much? Is it the trembling body? I would like to ask you a question. Do these people look relaxed when they are trembling and shaking? It sounds a ridiculous question but it is simply put to illustrate the point clearly. When someone is shaking, trembling and ill at ease they are clearly not relaxed. What caused this feeling? The alcohol of course. The addict then has some more alcohol and the shakes stop. The drinker now believes that alcohol helped him relax. The reason is because they are more relaxed than they were a minute ago but nowhere near as relaxed as they would feel as a non-drinker. This is because, even while they are drinking alcohol, they are still only partially suppressing the tense feeling that the alcohol caused in the first place. The more of the drug they take, the more of a withdrawal they will have; the more the withdrawal, the more they take to try to stop it. They have treated the symptom of the disease with the very cause and created a vicious circle. Until they remove the cause they will always suffer with the symptoms because they will always have the disease.

Even though nearly every drinker has suffered at least once from 'the shakes' (the morning-after feeling when you have had one too many), most of the time they are not aware that the body is in an almost permanent state of attempted recovery. It is when the body is recovering from the physical and mental pounding of the poison flooding the bloodstream that it becomes tense and for it to recover fully from this feeling will take anything from three to ten days. The average drinker rarely goes longer than four days without a fix. In order to see how part of the illusion works, we need to understand exactly what happens when alcohol enters the body.

Alcohol goes straight through the stomach wall without being digested, giving an instant rush of glucose to the bloodstream. This stimulates the excess production of the powerful hormone insulin. Any rush that you feel when you have alcohol is simply the insulin going through your blood trying to burn all the alcohol you have just put in. The insulin produced to deal with this actually causes your blood sugar levels to fall. When you feel the effects of low blood sugar, what do you need? A quick fix of course. The moment the insulin reaction has cleansed your bloodstream of this excess sugar, you are then running on empty. When you feel empty you feel tense but when you drink more alcohol you feel instantly more relaxed because you have loaded your bloodstream with glucose and momentarily suppressed that empty feeling. But again, all that has actually happened is that you have partially ended a low that the drug itself caused. A low that, for most of the time to the average drinker, is imperceptible. Now I understand how this accounted for my really low feeling on a Sunday morning after I'd been on an alcohol binge on Saturday. I would always crave a big fry-up and now I know why: I was suffering from hypoglycaemia or low blood sugar. This accounts for the fact that many drinkers eat a lot of sugary foods and why they run on nervous energy.

So, alcohol causes low blood sugar, drains the body of water, overworks the liver, pancreas and kidneys and leaches oxygen from the brain. That doesn't sound very relaxing to me. The truth is that alcohol does not really help anybody to relax. We tend to fix ourselves a drink at relaxing times like a lunch break, finishing work, having a long hot bath, finishing the chores, a dinner party or lying on a beach. The drink gets the credit but alcohol is incapable of creating a genuine feeling of relaxation. If you drink alcohol in situations that are not relaxing, will the drug create the feeling you crave?

THE DRUG NEVER CHANGES, ONLY THE EXCUSES WE GIVE TO JUSTIFY OUR INTAKE!

Did we start drinking to help us relax? Did our parents encourage us to drink alcohol before we took our exams so that we would feel calm and relaxed? They should have in theory. Come to think of it, we should all be encouraging children to have alcohol before they go into exams because that way they can feel calm, relaxed, confident, courageous and happy while tackling this unnerving task. If people genuinely believed that alcohol relaxes them, then why do bosses get so annoyed when their staff have had too many at lunchtime? Surely it is good to have a calm and relaxed workforce, isn't it?

If we believed our own hype about alcohol, let alone everybody else's, it would make sense to drink all the time. When you wake up with worries on your mind, why not have a drink to relax you? It would seem the logical thing to do if you genuinely believed that is what alcohol does for you. If you see a person being violent, the first thing you should do is give them a drink to relax them. Can you imagine a country where over 80 per cent of the population was taking a drug regularly that helped keep them calm and relaxed? Wow, you would have little or no crime in such a society. It would be the calmest and most laid back nation in the world. We can but dream of such a place.

The President of the United States should be advised to drink alcohol regularly as, to be a world leader, he should be confident, courageous, relaxed, strong and dominant wherever possible. Remember Boris Yeltsin who always looked the picture of happiness and courage? He always looked very calm and relaxed, don't you think? Relaxed? He could barely stand up because of the amount he had been drinking. That is not relaxation, it is being drunk, and there is a big difference. He could hardly run a bath let alone a country!

You are never genuinely relaxed when drinking alcohol. When a heroin addict is lying on the floor do they look relaxed or totally 'out of it'? When you see an alcohol addict collapsed in a heap on the floor do they look genuinely relaxed or 'out of it'? 'Out of it' means just that, or void of any genuine emotion and unable to relate properly to their surroundings. People also try to argue that alcohol is an anaesthetic. This is true, but being anaesthetised does not mean being genuinely relaxed. Heroin is also an anaesthetic, in reality a more powerful one than alcohol, but would you take heroin to help you to relax? And would it really relax you anyway? Do you believe that a heroin addict is more relaxed than a non-heroin addict? If you were having a nice relaxing jacuzzi with a person who had just taken some heroin, who would be relaxed and who would be tired and zombified?

When a powerful poison like alcohol enters the bloodstream, the body has one of two options. It can either store it or get rid of it. Alcohol is so poisonous to the human body that it cannot be stored for very long or you would die. This is why your body expels all the alcohol within the first week to ten days. It has no choice but to get rid of it for its survival. Alcohol is removed by the liver at a rate of one unit per hour; this process cannot be speeded up by drinking coffee or anything else for that matter – that is yet another fallacy. This process takes up so much energy that your muscles, bones, in fact everything feels tired and heavy, or relaxed as we have been conditioned to say. The reality is that your body is a long way from genuine relaxation as it is getting a pounding from a poison. If you pass out on alcohol it means that your body cannot keep you alive and awake at the same time as it needs all its resources to deal with the poison in the bloodstream. When you lose the use of your sight, hearing and consciousness you are effectively in a coma. Being comatose is not relaxation.

The addict, however, remains blind. I certainly did. In order to want to feel relaxed you must be tense to begin with. Why are drinkers so tense? I couldn't relax properly even at a social gathering if for some reason I wasn't allowed to drink or I had to control my intake. There is nothing more stressful than being a slave to a drug. We never seem to be aware of the mental and physical slavery we suffer. Of course I was tense and found life tough. I was permanently below par because I was dependent on a drug. Sometimes I would snap at people when I'd had a drink; also when I couldn't have one. If I was drinking I was 'under the influence' and if I couldn't drink I was 'under the influence.' I would feel deprived and that would make me tense, just like a child who, when told they cannot have a toy, throws a tantrum. It is exactly the same with the deprived drinker.

'Give them a drink to steady their nerves.' We hear that all the time, but what does alcohol do? It destroys the central nervous system. The only nerves that alcohol can steady are the nerves of somebody who is already suffering from alcohol withdrawal. Even then it only alleviates the unsteady nerves temporarily as it caused them in the first place. When you see a person smashing a broken glass into someone's face in a pub would you ever, even for a second, think 'I know what they need to steady their nerves; I'll get them another drink'? When somebody is shouting obscenities after having had a drink you would never think of giving them another drink to calm them down! Why not if you believed alcohol to be a genuine relaxant? Give them enough alcohol and they will eventually pass out but, again, that is not true relaxation.

Alcohol has even found its way into outer space. The Russian *Mir* space station is apparently partly fuelled by vodka. Not the station itself but the Russian cosmonauts on board. American astronauts arriving for duty on board the Russian craft were said to be amazed and flabbergasted to be offered a stiff vodka to calm their nerves after a tricky spacewalk. It is said that one particular Russian spent his time aboard *Mir* completely out of his head, or totally spaced out! Why didn't they have a drink before the space walk so that they could feel relaxed for that tricky task? Because they would be dead by now.

So the conclusion is that alcohol does not help genuinely to relax at all and that this feeling is another fallacy. I also mentioned in this chapter that alcohol destroys your courage and confidence; surely I am not suggesting that alcohol doesn't give people a little bit of the good old ...

Dutch Courage

YOU CANNOT BE COURAGEOUS
WITHOUT OVERCOMING FEAR.

Not only am I suggesting that alcohol does not provide any genuine courage or confidence but I am categorically stating that it does the complete opposite. Alcohol destroys your courage and your confidence and this is the most damaging part of the whole con trick. One of the biggest advantages of being free is getting that true confidence and courage back.

When you see somebody of five foot nothing and built like Kate Moss taking on Arnold Schwarzenegger after they have had a drink, does anybody think for one second that they are being genuinely courageous? No, everybody but the addict thinks they are stupid. Alcohol removes our natural fears so we feel a false sense of confidence and courage. If you do not have any fear, you simply cannot be courageous. A courageous act can only happen when there is fear to overcome. How can you have any genuine courage if you don't feel fear? When you see Tom having a go at the waiter after having a drink, do you look back in admiration and say, 'I never realised that Tom was such a confident man' or do you want to apologise profusely and say, 'Please ignore Tom, it's just the drink talking'?

The truth is that the person on the outside is never fooled; however the addict, in this case Tom, is. Even when Tom wakes up, he is still fooled into believing that the way he felt the previous night was genuine. So an easy way for Tom to gain confidence and courage is to drink alcohol again. The problem is that it is all false. Some people question whether it actually matters if the feeling is false because as long as the addict believes it to be real, then there is no harm in it. Yes there is. There is tremendous harm in removing your natural fears to give yourself a false sense of courage and confidence for two very important reasons.

First, when we remove our natural fears, we become unprotected and vulnerable to all kinds of danger. We disable our most powerful survival mechanism. We need access to all our senses in order to react at a moment's notice. If we are relaxing and a door slams, we jump. We are meant to jump as who knows what danger there might be. Someone relaxing on alcohol will often be unaware of danger as their senses are numbed.

There are products commonly referred to as 'date rape' drugs. These drugs put the intended victim into a zombified state so they do not know what they are doing or where they are. All their senses become numb and the natural fears that exist to protect against such circumstances are removed. Sound familiar? We need our natural protective fears. Without them we put ourselves in the position of being both deaf and blind to the dangers around us. Sight, hearing, smell, taste, touch and instinct are all there for a good reason: to help us survive. Remove them and we lose the ability to access the adrenalin, the fight or flight hormone, and we literally become helpless.

Two teenagers who are about to fight may feel brave but, at the same time, they are probably hoping that someone will stop the fight before it's started. Even if the fight goes ahead, usually the second that one of them goes down, the other will stop and is considered the 'winner.' The worst that tends to happen is a bloody nose or two. However, give them alcohol and you remove their natural protection from hurting others or being hurt themselves. The only time you might see somebody getting kicked repeatedly in the face, even when they are unconscious and have blood pouring out of them, is when people are 'high' on drugs. The most horrendous violence is usually drink related. Those doing the kicking are not being courageous because their natural fears have been removed and they are out of control. The person lying on the floor would probably never have been involved had they been fully compos mentis and able to judge the situation.

When a young girl is walking back alone from a night-club she is meant to be slightly nervous and alert. Anything could be around the next corner and she needs her wits about her. Alcohol removes those fears and replaces them with a false sense of confidence. At times like these you do not want confidence, false or otherwise; you need your natural fears to keep you alert to danger.

Second, and I believe the most detrimental problem with this false sense of courage, is that the addict actually believes it is real. All the time alcohol is depressing the central nervous system and doing the opposite to what the addict believes. So while the addict is 'under the influence,' not only is the alcohol giving them a false sense of courage or confidence, but it also renders their own inoperative. As a result, their true courage will be suppressed and confidence so much that, eventually, they will be convinced they have no confidence without their 'fix' as they are so dependent.

In the film *The Wizard of Oz*, the lion had lost his 'C-c-courage.' At the end of the film he found it again. The truth is that he always had his courage. He never lost it at all; he just hadn't used it for a long time. The longer he went without using it, the more he was convinced that he had none. That made him more and more fearful, thus reinforcing his belief. How did he find his courage in the end? By having a drink of alcohol? No, of course not. Do you think that there is one person in a million who saw the film and thought the lion could regain his courage by drinking alcohol? No! He found his courage the very second he used it. When he felt that natural fear, he broke through it and rediscovered his true courage. If he had taken alcohol he would have had a very false sense of confidence and would never have found his genuine courage. Why look for something when you believe you have already found it? (Think about it.)

The drinker strongly believes that alcohol helps give him confidence and courage, but it's an illusion. The longer he believes it, the more afraid he is that he cannot live without the drug. I used to believe that you had to be a really confident person to live without alcohol but why did I think something as ridiculous as that? I never thought I was being confident or courageous for not taking heroin in order to enjoy or cope with my life. I never thought that I was a confident person because I was living without the need for LSD or crack, but to the person who is dependent on these drugs life could never be the same without them. They believe that those who do not take the drug are just confident people who do not need anything to bolster them up. They blame their personality or genetic make-up when it's actually the drug itself that is suppressing their true identity. As I will repeat over and over again throughout this book, the drug causes the need for the drug.

I felt as though I did not have the courage to do something as simple as stopping drinking alcohol. The fact is that I'd always had my courage but, just like the lion, I hadn't used it for a while. What was stopping me? Fear caused by the drug itself and the fact that the longer I took it, the more fearful I became. The more fearful I became, the more alcohol I drank to overcome those fears. But it's always the alcohol that causes the fear.

> ... the drug causes the need for the drug.

Children have fears but they break through them using their genuine courage. Look at children at birthday parties: they sing, dance, play and don't care about making fools of themselves because they are alive and having fun. Alcohol addicts are even afraid of doing that. They believe that in order to have fun you need a drink first. Every time you overcome a fear you grow as a human being; if you are not growing you are dying, there is no in-between. This, I believe, is the saddest part of alcohol addiction. The more you depend on alcohol, the more convinced you are that you cannot cope or enjoy yourself without it and the quicker you die inside. Then your life is less fulfilling and when this happens, the more you rely on alcohol to fill that gap. This is why I was so afraid of stopping. I always thought there would be a permanent gap in my life if didn't drink. It is alcohol that creates the gap and getting rid of alcohol fills it. Now that the gap has been filled just the thought of drinking again fills me with fear, not the other way around. Why should we fear not drinking? That should be the real question.

Alcohol destroys your courage and confidence. What confidence or courage do you need to eat a meal with friends? What courage do you need to lie on a beach, enjoy a party or talk to people you already know well? Why should you ever feel insecure on these occasions? Exactly what confidence is needed to watch the football, go to a wedding, a christening or even wake up in some cases? There are people who have already reached the bottom of this pit, 'skid row' as it is commonly known. These people cannot even function without a drink in the morning. Do you think that the drink is helping them get through another day or has the drug itself buried their true confidence so much that they now believe it only exists inside a bottle?

'But I would never reach that stage because I am not an alcoholic,' I hear people say. There is no such thing. You are in quicksand; you are living the lie. Your confidence will not improve with alcohol; it will slowly wither away as it has been doing for years. This will happen imperceptibly. This process is often so gradual that you will put it down to all kinds of other things like your job, family or lifestyle. I reached the stage where I couldn't go to any social gathering or cope with any stress without having a drink beforehand. I was just like any alcohol addict; my true confidence had been suppressed. I just didn't know how to enjoy myself without a drink. All I knew was that I was miserable and happier when I had a drink. Foolishly I concluded that I was happy because I was drinking but that was never the case. I see it all very clearly now as I go out more than I ever did and have more confidence now than I ever had in my entire adult life.

I used to delude myself into thinking that I didn't need to drink. I believed I was in full control of my intake and that I could take it or leave it. Yet I was aware that I had to control my drinking as I had to permanently watch my consumption. This is not control; this is slavery and this is dependency. When you are dependent on anything it slowly destroys who you are. It wears you down and drags you down. This is how alcohol really destroys your courage and confidence.

Trying to keep control of something that is actually controlling you is extremely soul destroying, especially when you believe that you are the only person having to do this. After all, everybody else is telling you that they are in control, that they drink because they choose to or that they might drink a little too much on occasions but it's not like there is a problem. But what are you telling everybody else? Are you telling them the same thing? The biggest problem is the constant battle to try to keep control of something that is in fact controlling you. It is very easy to tell if somebody is not really in control; it is when they tell you that they are. It sounds like a contradiction in terms but let me explain. When someone thinks it's a major achievement if they haven't had a drink in a week and brags about it, it means they are out of control. Why do people congratulate others who have managed to stay on the wagon for a couple of weeks, especially when they say they get genuine pleasure from drinking alcohol? What is so clever about stopping something for a week that you claim to be in control of? If you were in control why brag? It just doesn't add up. If I went a week without a drink I would tell everybody. All the time you hear drinkers trying to justify how little they take, yet bragging about how they can drink anyone under the table. If you are happy and proud of yourself because you have managed to go a week or more without alcohol the simple fact is that the drug is controlling you and you are not in charge.

There are people who go on the wagon to prove they are not hooked. As I mentioned at the start of this book, there is even a book called *How to Give Up Alcohol for a Month*. It states that you should stop for a month every year to prove that you are in control. The author also says that it will be very hard to do and that you will miss alcohol all the time and even suggests a day-to-day planner so you know what day you are on. So, stopping drinking for a month, counting the days and missing it all the time, would apparently prove that you did not have a problem with alcohol. But surely this would simply confirm your worst fears: that you do have a problem and that you are not in control. What does that do to your genuine confidence? Like everything to do with this trap, it shatters it. Think about that for a moment. If you were in control you would never need to buy a book like that in the first place, you would just stop. If I wanted to stop eating bananas and went around telling everyone who would listen that I had not had a banana in weeks and at the same time I was reading a book called 'How to Stop Eating Bananas for a Month,' wouldn't you immediately know that I had a real banana problem? Not only that, you would make absolutely certain that I sought help immediately!

As the drug suppresses your confidence more and more, the ability you may have had to exercise control between drinks reduces. Like all drug addiction, the more it drags you down, the more you will be fooled into believing that it's your last pleasure or crutch and the more dependent you will feel. But, as I have stated, the whole process of stopping drinking is easy and enjoyable. It's only the fear of stopping drinking forever and the belief that you will be missing out for the rest of your life that causes people to feel stressed at the very thought. After all, fear in itself is a stressful emotion. This is why people who stop, even for a couple weeks, get very uptight and stressed. It's not the physical withdrawal, but the feeling that they are missing out. The problem is made worse because drinkers have taught themselves and been brainwashed by society to believe that alcohol relieves stress. So the more deprived they feel, the more stressed they become and the more stressed they become, the more they will crave a drink. It is only the mental craving causing the stress. The irony is that, contrary to what you have been brainwashed to believe and what you might think at the moment, alcohol is incapable of relieving genuine ...

Stress

If you tell a lie long enough and hard enough, even the person telling the lie will end up believing it. This is exactly what has happened with the conviction that alcohol relieves stress. Alcohol might block your mind to some of your stress, but genuinely relieve it? Never! When the drug has worn off you still have the stress to deal with. It doesn't just go away because you blot it out. We, as intelligent human beings, tend to laugh at the ostrich putting its head in the sand, thinking that the danger has gone because it can no longer see it. By thinking that alcohol relieves stress we are doing exactly that.

Every time you wake up after drinking, you are physically, mentally, emotionally, socially and financially worse off than if you had not taken the drug in the first place. *That* will make you more stressed. The genuine stresses you had the day before seem much worse and now you are convinced that your life is very stressful. You never really put it down to the drink but if you are always trying to get over the physical and mental effects of a poisonous drug like alcohol, then you will always have an additional stress. Just the physical effects of alcohol take at least three days to get over. Alcohol addicts think that if they have had a 'skinful' on a Saturday night and a couple on the Sunday then they are fine by Monday morning. However, this is simply a level that they are used to. This is their normality.

There is only one stress that an alcoholic drink is even partially capable of relieving and that is the stress caused by the last drink. Even then it doesn't do that. Some drinkers near the bottom of the quicksand think 'at least it ends the stress of my need for a drink.' Does it? Or did it create that stress as well? I can recall numerous occasions when I was going to have just one drink and ended up having two, three, four or however many it took until there was no more or until I collapsed, whichever came sooner. Was I happy in this state? Was I calm? Was I stress-free? I don't know because I wasn't there to enjoy it. My senses were numb; I was stupefied and 'out of it.' While you are in this state, you remain vulnerable, unprotected and have your head in the sand, yet people take the drug because they believe it makes them more courageous, confident, calmer, relaxed, happier and stress-free. Alcohol never relieves stress, it does precisely the opposite.

> Alcohol never relieves stress,
> it does precisely the opposite.

Have you ever felt stressed when you are having a drink? Have you ever been uptight or argumentative while 'under the influence'? Ever got aggressive, obnoxious or loud when inebriated? Have you taken things out of all proportion or just been plain rude, spiteful or hurtful when you've been drinking? I really don't need to ask these questions as I know you have and you know you have. Everyone who has drunk alcohol has experienced some, if not all, of these emotions when inebriated. If we have been stressed at the same time as drinking alcohol why do we believe that it relieves stress? It is because, just like the heroin addict, we feel better when we first get our fix. Also we have ended the 'wanting' a drink feeling created by the belief that it will help the situation, while at the same time partially suppressing the physical low created by the drug itself. However, this is just one of the many excuses we use to justify our intake.

Either the offender or the victim (or both) has been drinking alcohol in 65 per cent of murders and 75 per cent of stabbings in the UK. Do you think these people were stress-free? Do you think 'It's a good job they had alcohol in their system to relieve some of their stress, otherwise God knows how many people they might have killed'? Of course you don't because you know that these crimes happened largely due to the depressant, alcohol.

When I was a drinker I was always more stressed than I am now. I was either on the drug, thinking about when I could take it again, trying to control my intake of the drug or coming off the drug. Non-drinkers just do not have these stresses. I don't have them any more. I used to get stressed whenever I heard the bell for 'Time Please' in the pub. I may already have had five pints with one more sitting in front of me, yet I still wanted more, why? Was I stressed? Was I unhappy? Was I not being sociable? Wasn't I relaxed? Did I need courage?

Did I need confidence? No, no, no, no ... I just needed more of my drug like any other drug addict. I felt a chemical reaction that simply made me want more and more. I would walk to the ends of the earth to get more. I would pay any amount of money for 'take outs' as money is never an issue when you have been chemically and mentally programmed to need a drug. That is why, no matter what the cost, when you are 'under,' you don't care. This is when you can see clearly that it's a drug addiction because, at these times, you would drink sewer water provided it contained alcohol.

If the car engine blows up, you can consume a thousand alcoholic drinks but you still need a mechanic. If your partner leaves you, all the drinks in the world will not bring them back or help you find another one. In reality it does the opposite and it probably drove them away in the first place. If you are looking for someone new, you might recognise this remark: 'I have never gone to bed with an ugly person, but I have woken up with a few.' Alcohol really does change your perception.

Alcohol causes financial stress, physical stress, mental stress and emotional stress. Exactly how does it relieve stress to wake up worrying about what you have said and done the night before or how you got home? Where is the relief in wondering how you can face people thinking: 'I really didn't mean to do it,' 'God I wish I hadn't had so much to drink, I have a very important day ahead,' 'I'd better not drive this morning, I think I am still over the limit' and 'How much did I spend last night – where has all my money gone?' Then there are the even more embarrassing questions: 'How did I get here?,' 'Who are you?'

People who do not drink simply do not have these stresses. It is only the people who do drink who are stressed out by alcohol. When I was stressed and still an addict, I would say 'God I need a drink!' I would then phone a friend either to join me for a bottle at home or go to a pub. As the evening progressed I would start to feel better. Why? Was it because the alcohol helped put things in perspective or was it because I was able to talk about my stress with a friend? Alcohol alters your perspective. Again the addict remains blind as, to them, it was the alcohol that helped, not the friend. However, the biggest stress is having constantly to control your intake. I now do not have that stress. Nor do I wonder when I can have my next drink without having to exercise control or the stress of having to keep it to just a couple because of work or whatever. I don't have the stress of feeling resentful about not drinking because I have to drive people nor do I have the physical, financial, mental or emotional stress that alcohol dependency creates.

Once again, children provide the best example. If your child was stressed because she had too much homework or was being bullied at school, would alcohol help her stress? So why do you think that it would help yours? It's for the same reasons that I did because it appeared to help at times. Any outsider can see clearly that alcohol, far from relieving stress, causes it. Alcohol causes both physical and mental aggravation that, in turn, creates various degrees of stress. Any form of aggravation, whether physical or mental will affect your ability to focus or concentrate properly. But there are some drinkers who believe the illusion that a drink helps them to …

*Con*centrate

This is yet another clever con trick. Any form of concentration takes mental and physical focus. If you have an aggravation, like feeling the physical effects of coming off a drug or experiencing mental dependency on drink, then you will not be able to concentrate as well as you would without these aggravations. If somebody is suffering from the DTs they feel as though they cannot concentrate without a drink. The fact is, the only reason they cannot concentrate is because of the drink. In order to concentrate on anything at all you must first get rid of anything that is aggravating you. A heroin addict cannot concentrate properly without their drug. When they take the drug they are calmer and more relaxed and so better able to concentrate, but is there one non-heroin addict in the world who believes that heroin helps people concentrate? When I was on the wagon for three months I couldn't concentrate properly at any social gathering. Even though the physical aggravation had gone, I still had the permanent mental aggravation of wanting to drink.

Some people have built up such immunity and tolerance to the drug that the withdrawal effects have become normal and they believe this is how they are meant to feel. The chemical reaction automatically sends a signal to the brain and the thought 'I want a drink' occurs. While they retain that thought, they will not be able to concentrate properly until they get what they want. Part of their focus has now been taken up with an urge caused by a subtle chemical reaction in the body. As soon as they fix themselves a drink they will be better able to concentrate. The funny thing is that, as soon as they take a sip, they will crack on with whatever they need to focus on, yet the drink has had no time to take effect whatsoever. It's psychosomatic. If the alcohol did take effect, they would definitely not be able to concentrate on anything. You need total concentration and focus to pass a driving test so why not have a drink before the test? Because it changes your judgement, slows your reactions and causes mental and physical aggravation. Do you think that Andy Murray would concentrate better on his game if he had a drink before a big match? Would children focus better on their homework if they fixed themselves a little 'Scotty' (Scotch) before they began? A brain surgeon really needs a steady hand and full concentration to do the job – alcohol to the rescue once more! What an amazing drug alcohol is, it does everything. Sorry, it appears to do everything and that is the con.

The only reason why drinkers are better able to concentrate at certain times when they do have a drink is because they are either ending a physical low (caused by the drug) or they have satisfied their psychological dependency on the drug. The truth is that they are only ending an aggravation. When you eliminate any aggravation you are better able to concentrate than you were but you shouldn't have had the aggravation in the first place. Think about it logically. How can a depressant that destroys brain cells, numbs your senses (including sight which is a valuable aid to focusing), slows down your reactions and stupefies you, help you concentrate? It can't. It is yet another con.

'But Jason, if you have nothing to do, at least alcohol helps to relieve ... '

Boredom

I've said that when we are doing something we instinctively know to be stupid, we have to come up with some rational reasons to try to justify it. However, this particular excuse really takes the biscuit. In my private sessions I often get drinkers telling me that alcohol helps when they are bored. Helps what: the boredom? Alcohol cannot in any way relieve boredom. In order to succeed we have to be honest with ourselves. If you are sitting by yourself and bored out of your head with a drink in your hand, you are still bored. When I was a child and I was bored, my mother would never say, 'Oh have a drink, son'; she would say, 'Go and do something.' Alcohol is a drug and, as such, creates a void and when you have a void in your life you can frequently feel bored.

The effects of the body trying to repair itself after you have taken the drug combined with the gradual suppression of the nervous system can also lead to boredom. After all, every minor task can appear to be a huge effort when you feel as if you have just been run over by a truck. You can eventually reach a permanent state of tiredness and lethargy so you just can't be bothered to do anything. If you have enough alcohol it will knock you out so I guess you are no longer bored but then you are no longer anything. Shooting yourself in the head would also knock you out and it would solve your boredom issues for life. The only way alcohol can relieve boredom is when you watch somebody who is drunk. You're not bored then because you know anything can happen. Alcohol is incapable of relieving boredom as, once again, it helps to create it.

If we look closely at some of the apparently rational reasons that are given to justify alcohol intake, not only does alcohol fail to do what we think but it does exactly the opposite. Most of the reasons we give completely contradict one another: 'It calms me down' and 'It livens me up.' How can the same drug help to solve the opposite problem? It can't, it is just another part of one of the cleverest con tricks ever devised.

> ... not only does alcohol fail to do what we think but it does exactly the opposite.

The truth is that alcohol does the opposite of what it appears to do. It causes mental and physical stress, mental and physical tension, mental and physical aggravation. It suppresses your nervous system, destroys your courage, undermines your confidence and keeps you a slave to the stuff.

'Yes Jason,' I hear you say, 'but I do not drink to help relieve stress or help with my boredom. I am just a social drinker and you cannot escape the fact that even if alcohol doesn't do anything else it is a tried and tested ... '

Social Pastime

I can easily dispute the 'fact' that alcohol is sociable because it is far from a fact. I suppose you could say that it is a social pastime if you change the meaning slightly. A lot of 'social time' will literally pass you by when you are a slave to alcohol. To refer to alcohol as a 'pass-time' would be a more appropriate description. Just think of all the happy evenings, nights out, weddings, christenings, parties, the intelligent conversation, the dancing, games, banter and the days you have missed because of alcohol. I am not talking about the times you missed when you were physically present but your mind was blown. I'm talking about the times you miss because you have to exercise willpower, discipline and control because of the drug. Often I would choose not to go out if I knew I had an important task the following day. I knew that if I did I would end up drinking more than I wanted or that I would feel deprived all night because I wasn't drinking, which would be just as bad, so I would stay in on my own.

The main problem with alcohol is that you are never yourself whether you are drinking or not. If you have to restrict your drinking because you are driving, for example, then you will not be yourself; you will feel miserable and deprived without that drink. However, if you drink, then you won't be yourself either. This is because it numbs your senses. In order to feel any genuine emotion you need your senses. Alcohol also slurs your speech which, if I am not mistaken, is an extremely valuable aid to being sociable. The drug also takes away all reason and common sense. It makes you overemotional, loud and occasionally spiteful and hurtful. It can turn you into an obnoxious, annoying, slurring and argumentative person which is certainly not very sociable. Alcohol stupefies you but, more importantly, it removes those very important checkpoints between your brain and your mouth. You know the checkpoints I'm talking about; those that check your thoughts and stop unacceptable ones turning into speech. I shall repeat this for your own protection as well as everyone else's. Alcohol removes those vital checkpoints. Consequently, no matter what comes into your head, no matter how obnoxious, rude, offensive or stupid, it ends up coming out of your mouth. You often end up talking complete and utter nonsense for hours on end; that is, of course, if the anaesthetic effect of the drug hasn't caused you to pass out altogether which may be a relief all round. Passing out is a wonderful *pass-time*.

> Alcohol removes those very important checkpoints between your brain and your mouth.

When I gave up alcohol I went to a lovely New Year's Eve party. It was a black tie do with some very close friends. Everything was set for a good sociable evening: good company, good food, great atmosphere, great music and a good reason for celebration – New Year. Also there was free champagne all night though; when I say free, I mean financially free, as there is always a price to pay for drinking alcohol. The first part of the evening was taken up with people asking why I didn't drink and I will cover this later as it warrants a chapter of its own. The drug alcohol (or champagne as it was specifically named that evening) helped to destroy the rest of the party for many people, many of whom, unsurprisingly, became very antisocial because of it. One person I know was slumped on the bar for most of the time and was actually asleep before Big Ben had chimed in the New Year. What exactly is sociable about that? Others were fine for the first couple of hours; they were talking, laughing, interacting and being sociable, as was I.

The reason most drinkers are apparently fine for the first hour or two is because our bodies are very clever survival machines. As we continue to drink alcohol week after week, our bodies think there is no choice but to take this poison. They will automatically build up an immunity and tolerance to ensure our survival. This means that we need more and more to get the same effect or illusion. This again is why our first ever alcoholic drink floored us and we now need a lot more in order to achieve the same result. The more of the drug we take, the more the body builds up an immunity to it and the greater the immunity and tolerance, the more of the drug is needed to achieve the same illusory effect.

So, at first, everybody was fine and sociable. Again, I must emphasise that it was not the drink that made them sociable. What made them sociable was being at the party and talking to people. I was being just as sociable without drinking alcohol because non-drinkers are just as gregarious. I watched this scenario continue for a little while but as soon as the alcohol started to really kick in, the inevitable began. It started off with 'I f_ _ king love you!,' then 'I f_ _king love you, you bastard!' Then it just turned into 'You bastard!' In the end, what was meant to be the best party of the year turned into an occasion where people became argumentative, aggressive, obnoxious or spiteful. Others present were very overemotional, tearful or jealous. There were people falling over, collapsing on the floor, slumped over the bar and on tables. Others were literally being sick. The ones who managed to stay upright talked rubbish or danced (well kind of) and were not aware of the evening they experienced anyway as the real person was no longer there. They missed out on one of maybe only eighty or ninety New Year's Eves they will ever experience in their lives. When asked the following day if they had had a good time, many said 'I must have, I can't remember a thing!' If you can't remember the evening, how on earth do you know if you had a good time?

The reality is that they were being sociable until the alcohol took effect but as soon as it did, they became antisocial. I was one of the only ones left standing and still wanting to dance at four in the morning. I wanted to be sociable but there was no one left to socialise with. Why? Because of the alcohol they had drunk. It is so obvious when you can see it objectively.

For years I was convinced that alcohol helped people to socialise, especially when they were meeting for the first time. I thought, 'Top up their drinks as often as possible to get everybody talking and get over that awkward period.' In reality, this doesn't work as there is still that awkward period and people do not interact just because they have had a drink. If you are shy and inhibited, alcohol will not solve that problem any more than an ostrich putting its head in the sand will remove danger. On the contrary, it will release your inhibitions and stupefy you so the gulf between the real you and the drunken shy person becomes even wider. In the past I have been to parties where I have been drinking alcohol but remained in the same place all night talking to a small group of people I already knew. Isn't that frequently the case? At social gatherings we tend to interact with the people we already know. Sometimes we talk to others, at a dinner party for example, but on the whole we usually head for people we are comfortable with and already know. Would I have been unsociable if I had been drinking something other than alcohol? Of course I wouldn't. If I was stuck at home moping because I was off the drink or feeling miserable at a social gathering because I couldn't drink for some reason then, yes, that would be antisocial. Again, it would have been the alcohol that caused these problems anyway as people who do not feel the need to drink do not experience them. If you do not feel mentally deprived, you will happily socialise, no matter what is going into your mouth.

There are non-drinkers who are very dull and boring, but then there are drinkers who are just as dull and boring. There will always be dull and boring people around as that is part of life and alcohol won't help them socialise but will have just the opposite effect. It will ensure that they become loud, idiotic, abusive and display all the other unpleasant symptoms that go with drinking alcohol. In the end it will guarantee they end up even less popular than they were to start with. All drug addiction appears sociable ... to the addict that is.

There is a park in Switzerland where heroin addicts are allowed to obtain heroin legally and shoot up. To them, the park is like a pub – the only legal heroin pub in the world. It is a way for addicts get their fix openly and at the same time socialise with other addicts. They go back to the same park day in day out. What would happen if they discovered that all of their friends were not going to the park that day – would they still go? Yes, of course they would. Not to be sociable but to get the drug. These addicts never go to the park for the atmosphere, the weather or the social life; they go for the drug. They feel better there than anywhere else, for everybody around them is doing the same thing. If there were only one pub where you could drink alcohol legally, you would go there, not to be sociable but simply to get your fix.

I have been into a pub by myself for a bit of peace and quiet on many occasions. I would get out my newspaper, have a drink and relax. I could have gone anywhere to do that, a library for example. It's a lot quieter there but I did not choose to go there for the simple reason that they do not sell alcohol.

Heroin addicts think that using heroin is sociable. Crackheads think taking crack is sociable. Alcohol addicts think drinking alcohol is sociable. I used to have such double standards when I was taking alcohol, as do most drinkers. I would say that alcohol is pleasurable and sociable but if someone was taking the drug at a different time to me, in the morning for example, I would immediately judge them. Don't the majority of drinkers do that? Don't all drug addicts do that? I needed to judge. It was a way of proving that I wasn't like them. In truth, it was simply a way of saying, 'Look everyone, this person is out of control of their alcohol intake whereas I am in control.' By pointing out what I believed to be their weakness, I was in fact trying to justify my own. It's the same with people who procrastinate all the time. Their life becomes a mess, but if they see that you have put off one little thing, they will immediately pounce and condemn you for your procrastination. You and I know that if someone is drunk and you are sober, you hate it. You don't think that they are being sociable, confident, courageous, jolly people. You think exactly the opposite of what the addict thinks. You think that they are being very unsociable, annoying and stupid and usually you can't wait to get rid of them.

If someone drinks eight pints in the pub, they are generally considered to be a social drinker. If a businessman downs half a bottle of Scotch every night, he is considered an alcoholic. If somebody downs half a bottle of wine with lunch, nobody says a word but if someone is lying on a bench drinking a can of beer, they have a problem. Most drinkers judge other drinkers. Why? To make themselves feel better of course. I used to say things like, 'Have you noticed how much so and so is drinking at the moment? She downed two bottles of wine by herself last night. I think she might have a problem.' But another time I would say, 'Do you know what I am going to do tonight? I'm going to run a nice hot bath, crack open a good bottle of wine and relax with a book.' If I had said that I was going home to drink a bottle of wine by myself for the sake of it, that would have sounded as if I had a problem but, by making it sound good, I could justify my intake of the drug. That is what all drug addicts do: they try to justify their own intake. Haven't you judged people because they happen to be drinking at a different time to what is considered acceptable? Have you ever criticised someone else for drinking too much? The drinker's attitude is often 'holier than thou.'

I have said that I drank to be sociable but what is sociable about drinking alcohol? Being sociable means interacting. How can you possibly interact with someone who has lost control of their senses? How can drinking alcohol increase your ability to socialise? It can't, it's yet another lie. The lie, or illusion, is created by the fact that you happen to be socialising while having a drink, consequently you believe that the drinking is sociable.

Not long after I'd stopped drinking I went to a place called Aberdovey in Wales, for a water-skiing weekend with friends. On the first night we all went to the pub and I was asked what my 'poison' was. I replied that I would like a pineapple juice and lemonade. The person buying the round responded by saying, 'No, come on, what are you having really?' I thought that the last thing I wanted was to get into a discussion about not drinking, so I simply said that I was driving. That still wasn't good enough, as my friend said that he was also driving and we could all leave our cars where they were and jump into the minibus they had ordered to take us back to the hotel. I then explained that I wanted to start off with a soft drink. Everybody then started to comment and ask what I intended to have after that. In the end I was forced to tell them that I didn't drink alcohol any more. I really don't know what reaction people get from their heterosexual friends when they tell them they are gay but I can only imagine that it is similar to telling people that you have stopped drinking. I had absolutely no idea how much interest and disbelief that this 'admission' would cause; I felt as though I had just come out.

Inevitably the first question was, 'Oh I didn't realise that you had a drink problem – are you an alcoholic?' The question appears obvious as we have been conditioned to believe that if you stop drinking for good it can only mean one thing: you have lost control and are an alcoholic. This question is ridiculous when you analyse it. I don't drink any more, so how could I have a drink problem? The irony was that they were drinking alcohol (taking the drug) while asking me if I had a drink problem. You would think it odd if a heroin addict took heroin in front of you, offered you some and because you refused, commented, 'I didn't realise that *you* had a problem with heroin – are you a heroinoholic?' How absurd would that be? Who would you, or in fact anybody, think had the problem? You really don't need to be Sherlock Holmes to work it out do you?

My friends in Aberdovey reacted by saying things like, 'Come on you boring bastard, what's the matter with you, you antisocial git?,' 'Go on, let your hair down, we are here to have fun' and so it went on.

Just when did I become boring? At what point had I become antisocial? When did I say that I wasn't going to have fun? Just before they asked me what I wanted to drink, we were in the same place, talking, having a laugh and being sociable, so what had changed from the moment that I said that I didn't drink alcohol? I was still the same person; I was happy, not boring and being sociable because I was out with people. The only thing that had changed was that the drinkers could no longer take their drug without having to think about what they were doing as I was no longer a co-conspirator. Hardly anybody who takes alcohol thinks about it when they are in a room full of people taking the same drug. They are, after all, telling the same lies and believing them. I realised something that night that I had never understood until that point.

When I smoked and saw people around me who had stopped, I would envy them because I wanted to be like them. I knew that all smokers would love to stop given the choice and that all smokers envied non-smokers but I never thought that would apply to alcohol. Even when I was drinking and saw people who had given up or stopped for a while, I never envied them; in fact, there was a part of my brainwashed mind that actually felt sorry for them. I was, after all, suffering from the delusion that they were missing out. The real problem was that they were too. That is why I didn't envy these people when I was drinking; they were miserable and depressed because they couldn't drink. They were pining for a drink and feeling deprived. Why on earth would you envy people like that? There is nothing to envy about feeling miserable, uptight and depressed. As this is the image we have of people who don't drink, no wonder we are scared of giving up. Unlike smoking, of whom there are now literally millions of ex-smokers who don't miss cigarettes, people who stop drinking still feel as though they have made a sacrifice.

However, there I was, in a pub of all places, being sociable, laughing, talking, interacting, dancing, having a good time, not moaning because I didn't have a drink but actually feeling elated because I didn't have to drink any more. I never realised that this presented a totally new image of me. This was why they started to envy me as they began to realise that I was still being sociable and doing everything I had before except drinking, and that I was not being a bore.

When you take a drug of any kind and somebody else isn't, you start to question why you need it and they don't, especially when they are happy without it. These friends started by saying I was unsociable, boring and had a drink problem but finished by questioning their own drinking habits.

I digress slightly. I will return to 'other drinkers' in a later chapter. The point I am making here is that there is no such thing as 'sociable drinking.' When alcohol takes effect, you cease to be sociable, instantly. Being sociable means interacting with others and if you are doing this without consuming alcohol, you are still being sociable. What you shove down your throat doesn't make you sociable. The sociable aspect of alcohol is just another fallacy.

The sad reality is that a world in which alcohol is drunk by the vast majority of people would be a world of beatings, rapes, violence, arguments, obnoxiousness and overemotional behaviour. It would be a world of stress where true courage and confidence has been lost in a bottle or two; a world of suicides, murders and muggings. It would be a world of family hardship and abject poverty. That is what the world would look like if the majority of people drank alcohol. How do I know? Because it does.

I mentioned earlier in this chapter that there is always a price to pay for drinking alcohol, whether it's physical, psychological, social or emotional, but what about the financial cost? Have you ever really worked out how much money you will spend because you are hooked on the stuff? I know I never did but it is worth looking at, as it's anything but a ...

Liquid Asset

This fact will blow your mind, I know it did mine. The average drinker will spend roughly £100,000 on alcohol in their lifetime. Let me just repeat that as it is a bit of an eye opener. 'The average drinker will spend one hundred thousand pounds on alcohol in their lifetime.' That's a lot of money. Sometimes in my private consultations drinkers will say to me that they are not worried about the money, but why aren't we worried? Drug addicts of any kind constantly delude themselves. We can even fool ourselves into thinking that we have saved money on alcohol. For example, when you buy duty-free alcohol, you always think, 'What a result, I've saved thirty quid.' We are always talking about a saving and never an expense. How on earth have you saved money when you have just spent £30? It is still £30 more than a non-drinker spends. This is only an average figure; for some it will be a lot more.

I used to get through sixteen pints of lager a day at one stage; I was actually spending more on alcohol per day than I was being paid to work at the time. I would always wake up broke on a Monday morning. I would then have to sub some of my wages to pay for the next fix of my drug. I never saw it this way at the time; I was just a young lad who liked a beer and what was wrong with that? My wages at the end of the week were always pretty thin, as I had already drunk most of them the week before but when the weekend arrived it was always time to let my hair down and have a drink.

The situation changed slightly when I got a more professional job. I had more responsibilities so I had no choice but to control my intake. I was never really in control but felt as though I was. I wasn't spending more than my wages on alcohol any more (a major achievement) and was now a 'normal' drinker. I was spending as 'little' as everybody else. However, I never realised just how much drinkers have to pay in real terms to get their drug.

There is the direct financial cost that I mentioned, of course, but what about all the additional expense nobody ever thinks about that accompanies a dependency on alcohol? First there are the taxi fares. One of the biggest joys of being free is being able to drive my car whenever I choose; to go anywhere without having to worry about how or when I will arrive home. I used to pay good money every month for my car, yet during my leisure time I couldn't drive it because I was hooked on alcohol. I think back now on all those cold nights standing outside pubs and clubs drunkenly waiting for a cab. It would cost me a fortune to get home and the crazy thing was that I was paying for a car to sit my house. What about the times too when a cab driver refuses to take you home because you might be sick in his car and leaves you stranded? The average drinker will spend roughly £18,000, yes, eighteen thousand pounds, on taxis in their lifetime as a direct result of drinking.

Even before you get into the taxi, you may have the additional expense of buying food, or stuff that they tell you is food. As we all know, alcohol came first and kebabs second. The only reason that I would seek out a curry or kebab house with a restaurant at the back was simply to obtain more alcohol after hours. Again, the food is an additional expense. Next, you have the expense of losing money in your drunken state, possibly down the back of the seat in the taxi. You wake up in the morning with your head pounding away as blood is trying to pump through your dehydrated brain so you have to buy some more drugs to counter the effect of the drug alcohol; yet more expense. In addition, occasionally there is the cost of the flowers and cards to apologise for behaving like a complete idiot. Then you have the major expense of losing time at work. In the UK there are now eight to fourteen million working days lost each year as a direct result of alcohol. For some, there are repair bills either to their home where they have punched holes in doors and smashed things in the house or for damage to other's property. For some, it's the cost of losing their licence, not to mention the possibility of prison, or the fines for being drunk and disorderly. Many others suffer the huge financial cost of losing their jobs due to alcohol. The reality is that the financial cost seen in black and white is quite phenomenal.

I never really thought about the money because alcohol was my liquid asset and worth every penny, or so I thought. However, it was never an asset. Far from it, in fact. I was paying good money to be mentally and physically abused by a product that, in real terms, did absolutely nothing for me. It was all just a clever confidence trick. Just because millions of people are paying through the nose for something they believe to be genuinely beneficial, doesn't mean it is. Some 99 per cent of the population once believed the world was flat – were they wrong? Were they lying to other people by telling them that the world was flat? The answer is no. The world does appear to be flat. Even when you are flying around it your perception is still that you are flying in a straight line, isn't it? I have never been into space to check for myself that the earth is round but we now know for certain that it, is but doesn't this go completely against our own perception? In order to see the truth we have to move our minds beyond the appearance of something. Once almost everyone thought the earth was flat, except for one or two people. Christopher Columbus announced he was going to sail around the world and everybody thought he was insane. How can you possibly sail around something that is flat? Could he not see for himself the line in the distance that was the edge of the earth? Everybody else could easily see it, why couldn't he? People like Columbus and Galileo moved beyond the accepted thinking and opened their minds. As a result they got to explore and literally expand their horizons. They viewed things from a different perspective. The flat earth was just an illusion.

This book is all about changing your perceptions so you can see the truth. Alcohol does absolutely nothing for you at all. It only appears to give courage, happiness, confidence, relaxation and stress relief. But it's all an illusion. Those who open their minds and see it clearly can really explore who they are and expand their horizons. Columbus experienced a life that many were too frightened to pursue as they were afraid of falling off the edge. The only thing stopping those people was their false perception.

Even our government tells us that alcohol is good for us. Why do they keep perpetuating this blatant lie? Maybe it is because they are one of the biggest drug dealers in this country, if not the biggest! They are always talking about waging war on the drug pushers, yet not only do they allow alcohol to be advertised but they make a £8.5 billion profit (HMRC 2009) every year from a drug which is known to kill 9,000 people each year in the UK alone. I once watched a documentary which stated that half a million pounds is spent on alcohol each Saturday night in Newcastle alone. That really is something else!

As I've already mentioned, there are some people who are so brainwashed that they will spend hundreds or sometimes thousands of pounds on a bottle of wine. What plonkers (pun intended)! Sometimes I would justify the amount I spent on drink because I believed the biggest lie of all about alcohol which is that ...

A Little of What You Fancy Does You Good

This is without any doubt the biggest lie about alcohol. It's good for you!

Who tells us that alcohol is good for us? 'Experts' who are alcohol addicts themselves. But what does your body tell you? Wild animals have a very clever device to detect the difference between food and poison. It's their senses. We also have these incredibly clever devices. We do not need somebody with 'qualifications' to tell us what is poisonous; our senses will do that. It has only recently been recognised that smoking is incredibly harmful to the human body but a few years back the experts were telling us that smoking was good for us. It was usually these experts who were smokers themselves and that included many doctors. Perhaps they were attempting to justify their own intake of the drug?

When someone who has never smoked lights up a cigarette for the first time, they cough, splutter and can even be physically sick. What other health warning do you need? It is exactly the same with alcohol. When you had your first alcoholic drink how did your mind and body react? Didn't it make you feel physically and mentally sick? That is because it is a poison. Alcohol is a poison that destroys the entire central nervous system and increases blood pressure. It also destroys brain cells. Did you know that? Maybe you did, but have forgotten! When you drink alcohol regularly you literally pound the brain. It is rather like going into a boxing ring every weekend and deliberately hitting yourself on the head over and over again.

Is it good for you to destroy brain cells? Of course it isn't; the brain controls everything in your body and it tells your body how to work. If the brain cannot tell it how to work it will become sick. A nurse friend of mine told me that she was once present at a 'commando operation' on a man who had a tumour on the side of his face. It had spread so much that they had to remove virtually all the side of his face plus part of his head. This exposed his brain during the operation. The surgeon said that the man was obviously a heavy drinker and my friend asked how he knew. He asked her to look at its size which was a lot smaller than it should be. This, he informed her, was a direct result of the patient's drinking. So, alcohol actually shrinks the brain.

The experts tell us that alcohol is dangerous on the one hand but that, in small doses, it can be good for people over the age of forty. How did they come up with this? We hear this kind of nonsense all the time yet we never really question it. Why? Because it has been put across by the so-called experts. But does it make any sense at all? They say that alcohol can lower blood pressure and that it can also increase blood pressure. It either does one or the other. How can it do both?

Alcohol kills over 9,000 people a year in the UK, what is healthy about that? They say that the health gains are for people over forty who may be protected against heart disease yet over 80 per cent of people over the age of forty-five drink alcohol and heart disease is still the number one killer in the UK. If alcohol helped protect against heart disease, as is claimed, then we should be the healthiest nation in the world and our instances of heart disease should be almost zero. Kevin Lloyd, who played 'Tosh' in the television series 'The Bill,' died of heart failure, along with hundreds of thousands of people throughout the world, because of the alcohol he consumed. It is not good for you and, to say that it is, is a blatant lie. You don't need to take my word for it either, just look at the statistics. In the UK, 70,000 die each year from coronary heart disease. Add that statistic to the other effects of alcohol, which has been medically proved to:

- Depress your entire central nervous system.

- Undermine your courage, confidence and self-respect.

- Destroy your brain cells.

- Break down the immune system making you less resistant to all kinds of disease.

- Interfere with the body's ability to absorb calcium, resulting in bones that are weaker, softer and more brittle.

- Distort eyesight, making it difficult to adjust to different light.

- Diminish your ability to distinguish between sounds and perceive their direction.

- Slur your speech.

- Dull your sense of taste and smell.

- Damage the lining of the throat.

- Weaken the heart muscle and its ability to pump blood efficiently through the body.

- Inhibit the production of white and red blood cells.

- Weaken muscles.

- Destroy the stomach lining.

- Irritate the lining of the intestines, which in turn can cause ulcers, cancer, nausea, diarrhoea, vomiting, sweating, loss of appetite and loss of the ability to process nutrients and vitamins.

- Overwork the liver, kidneys and pancreas.

- Cause diabetes.

- Cause obesity.

In short, how can anything which is known to damage every single organ in the human body be good for you in any way, shape or form? The crazy thing is that all this information is common knowledge to the same experts who are telling us that drinking is good for us.

In fact alcohol is just as toxic to the human body as heroin. Let me repeat that as it is not a very well known fact. Alcohol is just as toxic as heroin. Are they going to tell us that heroin is good for us? Inebriation is called in*toxic*ation for a reason.

> Alcohol is just as toxic as heroin.

They even talk about sensible drinking limits. Sensible? How would you feel if they said that it wasn't sensible to get hooked and dependent on heroin but in small amounts it was sensible? Would you believe them? What really gets my goat is that they even brainwash us into thinking that people who drink small quantities are healthier than non-drinkers. This is rubbish, a huge whopper of a lie, but it's been repeated for so long that even the medical profession thinks it's true. They argue that alcohol can help to prevent blood clotting and, yes, alcohol does decrease the production of blood clotting agents. However, what they fail to tell us is that the blood is meant to clot otherwise we could suffer uncontrolled bleeding. Do you think that someone who takes heroin in small amounts is healthier than a non-heroin addict? Do you think that a body with small, regular amounts of poison is healthier than one that hasn't? There is no such thing as sensible drinking anyway. Have you ever seen anyone acting and talking sensibly when intoxicated? It's a contradiction in terms.

'But surely, if you drink for social reasons, then a little of what you fancy doesn't do you any harm, does it?' That is the same as saying, 'There is no harm in jumping into quicksand as long as you only go in up to your waist.' The nature of both is to drag you in one direction ... down. The only difference between the two is that one is quick and obvious, the other relatively slow and, to most, very subtle. There is no such thing as sensible drug taking. The only reason many doctors claim that alcohol is good for you and that the consumption of the drug is not an addiction is probably because they are hooked themselves. Virtually all doctors in the UK drink alcohol. I am not criticising them for this; they are in exactly the same trap that I found myself in and, because they cannot see it for themselves, they assume that there is no danger in taking alcohol in small doses. That is fine I guess because they may really have no idea that they are not in control, but to suggest that alcohol is actually good for you is nothing less than scandalous.

Why aren't we warned about alcohol before we start taking it? Why aren't there adverts letting everybody know that alcohol is a highly addictive drug with severe mental and physical side effects? Like everything else in this book, I want you to make up your own mind; but, remember, some years ago we were told that smoking was good for us.

Just because the body is clever enough to build up a tolerance to this poison doesn't alter the fact that alcohol *is* a powerful poison and a highly addictive drug. When you wake up after drinking alcohol do you feel good? When you see people vomiting in the street do they look healthier than someone who doesn't drink? 'Yes, but surely a couple of glasses of red wine a day, for example, can be good for you?' No it can't! The nature of any drug is to take more and more. Therefore when the medical profession makes statements like: 'A small number of units of alcohol a day is good for you but when you exceed our guidelines it becomes harmful,' they give the impression that people can control their intake. Surely they realise that we know just whose interests these statistics are serving? It certainly isn't the alcohol addict. I have already said that this is a fallacy as the drug always controls its victim, whether the victim realises it or not. The drinker regularly has to exercise resolve in order not to increase the intake. It only takes a very bad situation to occur in their lives and their resolve ends and the drinking increases. The more alcohol they take, the further down they go; the quicker they descend, the more they take. They end up in a downward spiral.

Sensible limits for alcohol vary throughout the world. Do people in the US have different insides from us? Can the constitution of a Scandinavian cope better with fewer units of alcohol? That is what we are led to believe when we compare the recommended daily intake of units around the world. There is only one safe limit for any drug that will damage and destroy you physically, mentally and emotionally, and that limit is the same level recognised throughout the world for every other mind-altering drug. No units at all.

In 1985, £100 million was spent treating alcohol related diseases in the UK. That sounds healthy doesn't it? I am not highlighting these health statistics to scare you into stopping because that rarely, if ever, works. I remember when I was drinking heavily, my doctor told me that my liver would pack up by the time I was thirty, so the first thing I did was to have a drink to calm my nerves. Little did I know at the time that it was absolutely not failing to calm me down. It was, in fact, doing the complete opposite. The reason for quoting these statistics is to underline the self-delusion that is involved in drinking and to help you see the product for what it actually is.

Everything I have just stated simply concerns the alcohol itself. I haven't even mentioned all the chemicals used to preserve it to make it appear drinkable. The chemicals used are too numerous to mention, but surely they cannot be good for us.

We are also told that if the damage is already done, then it is too late. What is? Is it ever too late to stop putting a poison into your body? Is it ever too late to cure yourself of a disease? It is certainly never too late to gain control of your life. The human body is, without doubt, a highly efficient survival machine programmed to keep you alive. When you stop putting a poison like alcohol into your body, it literally breathes a sigh of relief. No matter how long you have been drinking, when you stop your body will start to repair immediately. The body can do one of two things when a poison enters the system: either it can store it or it can get rid of it. It cannot store alcohol as, if it did, you would die, so it must get rid of it. The body wants to expel alcohol and will do so successfully as long as you don't put any back, which brings me to another part of the alcohol brainwashing process. Your body is incapable of craving alcohol no matter how long you've been drinking or your intake. Your mind and only your mind craves the benefits it believes alcohol offers. A craving is nothing more than an internal expression of the way you perceive a product; perceive it for what it really is and you will not have the craving.

> When you stop putting a poison like alcohol into your body, it literally breathes a sigh of relief.

I have mentioned that the physical and psychological slavery of drug addiction is bad enough for the victims themselves but there is one area that is rarely mentioned or addressed. It is the people who suffer daily from the very harmful effects of ...

Passive Drinking

We are always being told about the effects of passive smoking and frequently we hear about the crimes committed by heroin addicts, the houses broken into so they can fund their habit and the drug related shootings. But what about the daily misery that many people suffer as a result of passive drinking?

The late Roy Castle highlighted the effects of passive smoking. He contracted lung cancer as a direct result of other people's smoke. I am here to highlight the effects of a new phenomenon, one which causes more harm than passive smoking ever has done or ever will do and it's passive drinking. The sad truth is that there is hardly a single person who hasn't suffered or isn't suffering right now from the very dangerous consequences of passive drinking. This is the harm caused to someone as a direct result of another's drinking.

We often judge the person who drinks from morning till night on the harm they inflict on their family and others around them. There are support groups set up for the families who fall victim to passive drinking; the families who live with what society has labelled 'an alcoholic.' However, what we often fail to realise is the effect that all drinking has on other people. This includes the beatings, divorces, violence, neglect, the emotional as well as the physical hurt, sexual abuse, suicides, murders, stabbings, mood swings, outbursts, arguments, unwanted pregnancies, financial ruin, not to mention the pain, anguish and misery all caused by the effects of passive drinking which are second to none.

I once treated a young man for alcohol addiction. He had also been sold the idea that he was an alcoholic and was desperate to stop drinking. One of his reasons for wanting to quit was that he had beaten up his own father while under the influence only a few weeks earlier. He could hardly recall the incident and clearly would never have done it had he not been drinking. The reason for this was that it just wasn't him. He had been 'under the influence' of something that was controlling what he did and what he said. He was due to appear in court three days before Christmas. His father was not drinking but had suffered at the hands of somebody who had been – his own son. Not only had he suffered the physical harm but also the emotional hurt caused by his child because he was a victim of passive drinking.

A teenage boy woke up to find his best friend lying next to him in a pool of blood. He had stabbed him the night before but could not recall a thing. The boy was just eighteen at the time and had only been on a lads' night out. He blacked out because of the alcohol and is now serving a life sentence for murder. Was the murder drug related or was it even murder? Did he know what he was doing? He was not in control of mind or body as he was under the influence. Is this a true story? Yes. Is this a one off accident? No. Incidents like this are happening every day all over the world.

How many other people are now suffering from the effects of passive drinking because of this one incident caused directly by alcohol? First there are the families of both victims. The dead teenage boy and the boy who killed him are also victims. Their families' grief, sorrow and anger will be there every day until the day they die. The friends who have lost their companions and the people who lost their staff or colleagues also suffer. The paramedic who found the teenager's dead body would have to live with that image for the rest of his life and the boy who committed the 'murder' will suffer every day for the rest of his life. He will wake up each morning having lost his best friend and knowing that he killed him. Then there is the cost to the state of keeping him in an overcrowded prison for a crime he can't even remember committing. All this pain and suffering came about as a result of two boys wanting a fun night out. What possible harm could that do?

You may think that this is a very dramatic example and argue that in such situations there are many other factors, like the boy's personality, for example. Some people believe that you have to be 'that way inclined' in the first place; that you cannot simply blame such behaviour on alcohol. Yes you can. If someone commits a crime while on crack cocaine or heroin, people immediately say it's because of the drug and the perpetrators are offered help. However, if it's alcohol they get a prison sentence.

When somebody on LSD jumps from a roof believing they can fly, do we assume that it is in their nature to jump from roofs or is it more likely to have resulted from taking the drug? I have said and done many things that I would never normally do when 'under the influence' and so has every single person who has ever drunk alcohol. That is the nature of the beast. When you say things you would never normally say or do things that you would never normally do as a result of alcohol, inevitably, somebody close will suffer the effects of passive drinking. It is difficult to know just how many people are affected by this phenomenon.

Sarah Collins suffered so much from passive drinking that she took her own life because of it. Sarah is the unfortunate mother who committed suicide three years after a wine drinking session ended with the death of her daughter. She never recovered from the guilt of her six-year-old daughter drinking the wine that killed her. Stacey (her daughter) had so much alcohol in her body that her blood alcohol level was more than twice the drink-drive limit. This may sound shocking; you may even find yourself judging Sarah for what she did, but I was given wine with a meal as a child. In France it's seen as normal to give children a little taste of wine with dinner, albeit watered down. Sarah who was 'under the influence' at the time, was simply not aware that Stacey was going into the kitchen every five minutes to have some more wine, copying her mother, as children do.

The sad reality is that little Stacey would have suffered from the effects of alcohol long before she even took that first fatal drink. People are fooled into thinking that it's only alcoholics who neglect their families and cause heartache. However, the truth is that everybody who has ever drunk alcohol has caused other people either physical or emotional harm as a direct result of their drinking. Most of the time they will not even be aware of the distress they have caused but, in each case, the third party has fallen victim to passive drinking.

Children suffer all the time from the effects of passive drinking. They are frequently left to wait in the car with a Coke and straw while the adults go into the building for grown-ups only. They suffer the embarrassment of seeing their parents get overemotional, falling over or being sick. They see them getting loud, argumentative, aggressive or abusive to each other or towards them. They feel upset as they lie in bed at night, listening to alcohol fuelled rows or hearing the sound of physical abuse; memories that can affect their entire lives. There are the feelings of neglect and hurt when they cannot communicate properly with their drunken parents. They may desperately wish that they would return to normal so that they could talk to them and not to these 'other people' who they wish would go away. Children frequently suffer verbal abuse as a result of a parent's hangover and wonder what they have done to cause it. They miss outings because their parents have been drinking or have run out of money because of the cost of taking their regular drug.

> Children suffer all the time from the effects of passive drinking.

All children hate seeing their parents drinking, I know I did. There is nothing more embarrassing and upsetting to a child than their mother or father drunk. If you did manage to talk to your parents in their drug induced state, then you might either have them telling you how much they love you every two seconds or have them shouting abuse, blaming you for everything that has ever gone wrong in their lives. What's wrong with the first scenario? What is wrong with somebody letting you know how much they love you? If you have been there you will know exactly what is wrong with it; they are not telling you they love you because it's not really them. They are under the influence of a drug. This is not true affection, it's the drink talking and it's hurtful and embarrassing.

The majority of reported child abuse cases are directly related to alcohol. If a child has a parent on whom they depend and that parent is dependent on alcohol, then who can that child depend on? Obviously it's not just the children who suffer from passive drinking; the whole family feels the physical, mental and financial burden of having an addict in the family. These are just examples of people who suffer inside the home; there are many other people who are affected by passive drinking. Fifty per cent of all adult pedestrians killed in road accidents are twice over the drink-drive limit. That's not the driver, it's the pedestrian. The driver who knocks them down has to suffer for the rest of his or her life, blaming himself and desperately wondering what could have been done to avoid the pedestrian. They spend a lifetime suffering terrible guilt and regret even though they were not to blame. The accident and emergency staff suffer, not only through treating the patients who have been injured as a direct result of alcohol but also from the physical and mental abuse they receive from drunk patients who are the very people they are trying to help. Many hospitals now find it necessary to recruit extra security on Friday and Saturday nights. Ninety-eight per cent of physical abuse aimed at doctors and nurses is alcohol fuelled and the police also have to cope with an extra workload at weekends as a result of alcohol related incidents.

Then there are the victims of drunk drivers who suffer daily because of the effects of passive drinking. As well as the person injured or killed outright, families, friends and colleagues will be affected for the rest of their lives because of the tragedy. Then of course there are the other victims, the drivers themselves. The driver may wake up night after night in a cold sweat, reliving the moment over and over again and wishing every day that they could just turn back the clock.

Whole nations have suffered from passive drinking, including our own. England taught the world how to play football but was then banned from Europe for years because of the alcohol fuelled behaviour of its supporters. The 1998 World Cup in France erupted in violence incited by fans from many different nations, but mainly by those from England and Germany. Every single person arrested had been drinking. Was this a coincidence? Of course not. Alcohol is an evil drug that removes people's fear and causes death and destruction. A whole nation is suffering the effects of passive drinking. It cost English footballer Paul Gascoigne his life's dream, a chance to play in the final of a World Cup, as he didn't get to play in any of the games because of his drinking. The rest of the team were also the victims – they were being deprived of one of the greatest football talents of all time. It cost football legend George Best his life, even after he'd had a liver transplant.

If you are a non-smoker, you no longer have to suffer the effects of passive smoking at 30,000 feet as smoking is now banned on every major airline. However, even at 30,000 feet you can still be affected by passive drinking. It is now widely referred to as 'air rage.' British Airways have even had to incorporate a 'yellow card' policy for drunk and disruptive passengers after an air rage incident in 1998. Many passengers were in fear as a passenger went into a drunken rage. During one hour of mid-air mayhem he threatened to kill the pilot and headbutt a passenger, then he smashed a seat and indecently assaulted a stewardess. Staff and passengers had to wrestle him to a seat where he was handcuffed and strapped in by his ankles. Maybe they should have given him a drink to calm him down.

There are so many people who have been disfigured for life due to passive drinking. I was standing in a pub once when one man accidentally stepped on the foot of another customer. It's easily done but the next time I saw that man, he was lying outside the pub with his right eye resting on the pavement next to him. The other man had shoved a glass into his face for treading on his toe. The effects of passive smoking can take years to materialise but the effects of passive drinking are often instantaneous.

Every good night out on alcohol has a happy ending, doesn't it? When you think about it, you can usually look back at most events where alcohol is involved and laugh about them, can't you? After all, everybody knows that most nights on alcohol are just a ...

Barrel of Laughs

I always used to think that alcohol was a bit of a laugh. You can look back and laugh at some of the ridiculous situations that have occurred due to alcohol and, to be fair, some do seem quite funny. But are they? Is this just another way of covering up our stupid and destructive behaviour when drinking alcohol? Well, make up your own mind.

Alcohol stories tend to involve people making complete fools of themselves which turn into funny stories to be told over and over and over again. Over their drinking years people may only have about half a dozen alcohol stories anyway. The problem is that you hear them repeated again and again. Nearly all drinkers have at least one alcohol story up their sleeves; very rarely do they have more than half a dozen. It doesn't really occur to drinkers that they have told the same stories for years, that they have drunk alcohol for years and can still only think of a few 'funny' alcohol related stories. Actually, they are alcohol bores. I know that I used to do this but then alcohol does destroy brain cells, so maybe I just forgot that I had told the same stories a thousand times before. But were they ever funny in the first place?

I woke up one morning when I was just seventeen to discover that the night before I had run stark naked through my mother's house which was full of my friends.

I then went out into the middle of the road and tried to spin on my head. This was when break-dancing was all the rage. It was midnight and I was totally starkers. Funny? Well no, not really. I could easily have broken my neck and been confined to a wheelchair for life. Now that really would have made a funny story, wouldn't it? I have told that story for years with the usual 'Oh yeah, but guess what I did?' beginning. The truth is that I didn't remember a thing as I had a blackout. I have never forgotten the story simply because of the embarrassment that it caused me for years. Nearly, perhaps, as much embarrassment as the poor young man who woke up in the middle of the night to find himself halfway through urinating over his parents' feet as they slept in their bed. He was only awoken by his mother's screams and saw the look of sheer horror on his father's face. He was just sixteen at the time and ran away from home because of the humiliation. Funny though, isn't it?

For years I have told a 'funny' story about the night I stole (actually, borrowed for a little while) my uncle's van and was too drunk to remember that I hadn't yet learned to drive. I was in first gear all the way home. When I woke up, I remembered what had happened but couldn't get the van back as I remembered that I couldn't actually drive. When I looked at the van I could see that the front was smashed up and, as soon as I saw this, I began to experience flashbacks of the drive home. I remembered driving down a hill when a police-man tried to stop me by standing in the middle of the road. I swerved to avoid him and hit a bollard. How I actually managed to get home is still a mystery.

'Do you remember when I was so drunk that I fell asleep on the train and ended up in the middle of nowhere at seven o'clock in the morning with no money, cold and hungover? It took me all day to get home.' Funny? 'Do you remember when Peter drove the wrong way down a one way street and was too drunk to realise?' Funny? 'Yeah, but what about when Jill vomited in Nick's lap at that dinner party?' Hysterical? 'Yeah, but I've got a better one. What about when Tom was handcuffed to a lamp post stark naked and left out in the freezing cold for hours?' Hilarious?

There seems to be a real competition amongst drinkers to see who has the funniest alcohol story. I mean, you are just not a drinker until you have at least once forgotten where the toilet was and urinated in some outrageous place or vomited over your spouse's parents. Or until you have fallen off a balcony and cracked a rib, dropped off to sleep on a bus or train that was meant to take you home and ended up in a field lying face down in a cow pat. What about the time you slept with somebody who you thought was the picture of beauty, only to realise the next morning that you have in fact just slept with the creature from *The Hound of the Baskervilles*! Ever got the boot from work because you were too hungover to go in, or because one too many at lunch meant fluffing your work or being rude to a colleague or client? Remember the times when you called everyone in your phone book at 3 a.m. in your drunken and lonely state or fell asleep in the middle of having sex? Unless you have done at least one or maybe all of these you are just not a drinker. You see, drinkers try to justify their antics by turning it into a laugh whenever possible.

It's funny how drinkers don't sit around laughing about the arguments, the beatings, the violence, the abuse, etc. Frequently even the stories that were made into jokes were never funny in the first place as all too often there are consequences. The man who slept with the 'dog' from *The Hound of the Baskervilles* suddenly gets a phone call to say she is pregnant. The person who lost their way and ended up in a cow pat suddenly realises they have missed work again and have now lost their job.

Am I suggesting that I don't find some of these alcohol stories funny or that I have lost my sense of humour? No. Of course some are funny but seeing somebody trip over is amusing too. I once watched a friend of mine go to look out of a window but, because it was so clean, he put his head straight through the pane of glass. This isn't really funny but I can't tell the story with a straight face. (He wasn't hurt, in case you were wondering.) The point is that alcohol addiction is anything but a barrel of laughs. We laugh at some things that occur as a result of alcohol simply because they are about somebody who is out of control. The stories are simply part of the facade to justify drug taking. No doubt heroin addicts joke about how they once missed a vein and hit an artery. Funny? Or how they were so 'out of it' they nearly choked on their own vomit. Funny? The thing about alcohol stories is that they are told by people who can barely recall the event themselves and are simply telling you what happened afterwards or what others have described.

One of the biggest advantages to being free is the ability to remember everything, every part, every second of this very precious life and always to be in full control with the knowledge that you are seeing everything with a ...

Clear Head

Of all the joys of being truly free, one of the greatest is having a clear head at all times. When I have good time, I know it's genuine. I am able to remember the nights out, all of them. I can remember every conversation, every event, every minute of every day. I wake up and feel awake and alive. What a thought. I have found my true confidence and true courage. I no longer wake up wondering what I did the night before. I never ever have a hangover. Let me just emphasise that: I never ever have a hangover!

I am always refreshed, alert and energised in the morning. I have the genuine choice of fully utilising every single one of the precious days that we have while we are on this planet. I am able to drive my car whenever I want. I now have the freedom to go out every night without the worry of having to exercise control over my drug intake. I can go dancing until the early hours and still feel good the next day. I no longer have to spend my hard-earned money pouring poison down my own throat; a poison that controlled so many aspects of my life. I never have to take alcohol to enjoy or cope with my life. I no longer have to say sorry to people for my outrageous behaviour when I was 'out of it,' most of which I could never remember anyway. I suddenly have tremendous amounts of that most precious commodity – time. I never lose time because of the effects of either being on the drug or the mental and physical effects of trying to eliminate it. To me, every day is now as precious as the next. I have more money, much, much better health, more peace of mind, more self-respect, more courage, more confidence and tons more freedom. All of these are the benefits of a life free from alcohol addiction. The biggest gain of all is being mentally and physically free forever.

Someone in one of my sessions once asked me, 'If alcohol was free of charge and didn't do any harm to you or others, would you drink again?' The answer was without hesitation, 'No way, never, not in a million years.' They had to ask again, 'Did you mishear? I said if alcohol was free of charge and there were no health risks involved, would you drink again?' Again I repeated, 'No way, never, not in a million years.' The reason is because the difference is like night and day. It's the fact of the daily mental and physical slavery that never really occurs to drinkers. It's the having to drink in order to enjoy or cope with your life. It's the having to work your life around the time when can you have the next fix. It's the very lack of genuine freedom and real choice that never really dawns on drinkers.

I always said that I chose to drink and I believed that to be true but what genuine choice is there when you have to do something in order to cope or enjoy your life? It is freedom from this dependency that is the greatest gain. Most drinkers delude themselves into thinking that only those that society labels alcoholics have an alcohol dependency and have lost control. My point is that if you have to exercise control, you are dependent and are never really in control anyway. Why would you want to have this constant battle to exercise control over something that does absolutely nothing for you at all? That is why I will never drink again even if alcohol was free.

In the bad old days, every time I went to a party after a few in the pub, my first thought was not who would be there but to wonder whether there would be any drink left. If there wasn't, I would not enjoy myself. I couldn't, not without my drug. Before I spoke to anyone at a social gathering, I would have a drink. On many occasions I would not go out because I knew that I would drink. So I stayed in to avoid the temptation. If I didn't want to drink, why couldn't I just go out and not drink? It was because I was not in control and the drug dictated where I went and whether I enjoyed myself. That is dependency.

No longer to be dependent is one of the best feelings in the world. I relied on a substance that, in real terms, did absolutely nothing for me at all. I just couldn't see it as I was locked in a world that appeared real. If you see things from the outside it becomes incredibly obvious but if you are locked in a world that you are convinced is real, how will you ever know? The Hollywood actor Jim Carrey starred in a film that fooled his perception too. Let me explain a bit about the anything but ...

Truman Show

If you haven't seen this film, I will explain. I'm no Claudia Winkleman but please bear with me. Hollywood created the ultimate soap opera. The difference is that one of the characters in the film, Truman, played by Jim Carrey, has no idea that his whole life is being watched by the rest of the world, twenty-four hours a day. They call it *The Truman Show*. There are cameras in his house, his car, in fact everywhere he goes. Nothing is real in his world, not even the sea or the sky. All his family members are actors, including his wife. His workplace and home are just part of the biggest film set ever created. It is the ultimate voyeur's dream, a twenty-four hour live 'fly on the wall' insight into someone's life. It is the most watched television programme of all time and the makers are keen to keep it going for as long as possible. They are making millions out of controlling his existence and, if they manage to keep the illusion going until he dies, he will be none the wiser. Just like a real soap opera, there are scriptwriters planning what should happen next. Truman himself believes that the world he inhabits is real and every decision he makes is of his own choice and doing. Why shouldn't he? He has no idea that his life is being controlled and his very destiny is in the hands of a scriptwriter.

However, the makers of *The Truman Show* didn't take into account one eventuality. He wants to explore the world. The show is thirty years old and so is Truman.

There is a part of him that knows there is more to life than this and he wants to expand his horizons. This is a major problem as there is nowhere to travel and he lives in a world within a world but has no idea of this. The sea only goes so far and eventually hits the edge of the film set but how is Truman to know? The makers of the show do everything in their power to stop him even to the extent that Truman's father was killed in a fishing accident when he was a boy causing Truman to blame himself and be afraid of water ever since. In fact, his father was, like everybody else, just an actor who is really alive and well. The creator of *The Truman Show* had to think of something to stop him travelling so killing off his father this way seemed like a good plot device.

The next option for Truman was plane travel. However, when he went to the travel agents there were pictures of planes crashing to deter him. His actress wife is constantly telling him not to go travelling but to start a family. To cut a long story short, several events happen to make him sense that something is not quite all it seems in his world. He finally decides to cross the sea by boat, as there is just no other alternative. The director panics and creates a storm (literally) where Truman nearly dies. They cannot let him leave or let him die on live television. In the end his boat ends up hitting the sky which, after all, is just a large piece of heavy canvas. At this moment his perception begins to change. He climbs out of the boat and puts his hand on the sky. He then finds some stairs leading to a door in the middle of the sky. He opens it and realises he has discovered a whole new world he never knew existed. However, there is still fear.

Truman had only known his world and did not know what was out there. The illusions had been removed but there was a voice telling him that there was nothing out there that was not already here. The voice was that of the creator of the show making one last attempt to save his precious programme. Although Truman felt a little fearful, what was his alternative? Stay in a world where everything is false for the rest of his life? What kind of life is that? There really was no decision to make so he thought for a second and then, in a truly confident manner, he voiced his catchphrase, 'Farewell and if I don't see ya again, good afternoon, good evening and goooodnight!'

His life and destiny changed at that point and he became his own scriptwriter. For thirty long years everything he had believed was false. Just because he had firmly believed it to be real, did not make it so. Everyone on the outside knew it was all false but to one person in this artificial world it appeared very real. When the creator of the show is asked in an interview afterwards why he thought it took Truman so long to realise what was really happening, he replies, 'We accept the world with which we are presented.' How true is that?

For many years I firmly believed that everything alcohol appeared to do was real. I thought that it was all true. However, I was simply deceived but I was not the only one. I was accepting a world which I was being presented. In the film, Truman was the only person who was being deceived and controlled. He was just one person who was suffering from a delusion. When it comes to alcohol, there are millions being deluded around the world. I realised when I escaped that there is a whole new world out there. If you were Truman (let's say that you were not the only one being fooled but your whole family was being deluded), would you just watch from the outside once you discovered this whole new world, or would you do everything in your power to make everyone see that they also could be set free? You would want to do everything in your power to help them realise that they were deluded and trapped, wouldn't you? That is exactly how I feel. I can see it so clearly now and this book is about helping you to see something that is obvious when you look beyond the accepted perception.

The good news is that when you stop drinking you begin to write your own script and control who you are. You do not have to go through a storm of any kind, contrary to the brainwashing. There is a door in the sky that releases you to a whole new world and the key is in your own head; you are the master of your own show. The only thing that is stopping you is fear. I could have escaped years before but fear stopped me. In fact it was the false perception created by the alcohol itself and the conditioning since birth.

Another way to see beyond the false perception is mentally to step outside the cage for a minute and ask the question ...

Am I a Man or a Mouse?

A mouse is put in a cage and given food, water and a liquid drug. There is a button to the side of a metal funnel where the liquid drug is dispensed and, in order for the mouse to get the drug, it must hit a button with its nose. There is food and water but, out of curiosity, the mouse hits the button. The mouse has its first dose of the drug. It squeals loudly and its body reacts horribly to the poison in the same way a human does when experiencing its first dose of a liquid drug. The scientist then removes the food and water and the mouse is left only with the drug. Having no choice, the mouse then hits the button and drinks the liquid drug. After a while it goes back and hits the button again during the withdrawal period, in other words, as the drug is leaving the mouse's body. The mouse does not have the same reaction to the drug. This time it does not squeal and appears to have no adverse physical reaction to it. In truth, the mouse now feels slightly better than it did a moment before as the drug has now momentarily suppressed the feeling that it caused. The mouse has no idea but the liquid drug is designed to destroy its central nervous system. The mouse hits the button again during the withdrawal period and feels better than the moment before.

The scientist then puts the food and water back into the cage. The mouse takes some but then goes straight for the button. After a while the mouse ignores the food and water altogether and just continues to hit the button. In no time at all you start to see the mouse's body shaking. When it hits the button, it stops shaking and very quickly its nervous system begins to be affected again. When the shakes start again, what does the mouse do? Hits the button! Does the mouse feel better? Yes, but only better than it did a moment before and nowhere near as good as it felt before it started to push the button in the first place. The poor mouse has no idea that its central nervous system is slowly being destroyed by the drug and is tricking the mouse into thinking that it is helping. The more it shakes, the more it hits the button; the more it hits the button, the more it shakes. The mouse builds up such a tolerance to the drug that even when it hits the button it still shakes, just slightly less than before. After a while the mouse just continues to hit the button, hit the button and hit the button, until it dies.

This is an actual experiment routinely carried out in drug tests. I do not condone this type of practice but when I saw this experiment it dawned on me that this was exactly what I was doing when I was hooked. Once you hit the button a couple of times you really do become the mouse but, just like the mouse, you cannot see it while you are pushing the button. The drug appears to have the opposite effect to what it is really doing. The alcohol was suppressing my nervous system so much that in the end I believed I could not enjoy myself or be as confident without a drink. The insecurities I had were caused by the alcohol. It was the drug and only the drug that had done that to me. Now I am out of the cage it is easy to see. This book is about stepping outside yourself so you can see what is really happening. If the mouse had that opportunity to see what it was actually doing, do you think it would continue? The mouse doesn't have the rational sense to analyse its actions but human beings do.

So the question really is, are you a HuMan or a Mouse? Well then, it's time to …

Lose Your Bottle and Gain Your Courage

Just like the mouse and the scientist I now realise that I only had to look at other drunken people to know that alcohol doesn't actually do anything. But I was a mouse and under the influence. I believed in the alcohol world; a Truman-like world within a world. A world that had created a set of false fears to con me into thinking that I couldn't escape; a world that deluded me into thinking I could not enjoy life or manage without it. I had the bottle but had lost my true confidence. When I finally lost my bottle (and the can!), I regained it.

One of the greatest joys of being totally free is actually to be in a position where any moments of stress have once again become exciting challenges. As you are now aware, alcohol causes stress: physical, mental, emotional and financial. Because I am now physically, mentally, emotionally and financially much better off than before, I can easily deal with stress as it happens, instead of doing an impression of an ostrich every time a challenge comes along. More importantly, I do not have as much stress to deal with anyway. Once you are free you gain true courage and have true confidence again which means that you are a lot more capable of dealing with anything that happens. Stress only becomes stress if you are not strong enough to cope and, if you are slave to a drug like alcohol, you will always be more mentally and physically depressed than you ever would as a person that doesn't need to drink.

It is so wonderful to be able genuinely to relax with a totally calm and unstressed mind and body. No more effects of the drug itself, or stress of trying to get over the symptoms of the drug, or stress of feeling guilty because I needed the drug or stress of thinking about when I could next get it. Am I saying that you will never get stressed again once you stop drinking? No, of course not. There are good and bad days whether you are a drinker or a person who doesn't drink but, physically and mentally, you will be so much stronger that the highs will be that much higher and the lows nowhere near as low as they used to be. If somebody smashes into my car I don't say, 'That's OK, I'm a non-drinker,' I still get upset. The difference is that now I am much better equipped to deal with it and I do not feel the need to turn to a drug to solve that problem. I now turn to a mechanic. It's so nice to be the scientist and not the mouse.

The truth is that when you put your mind outside the cage you soon start to see the obvious. The only reason why the mouse was hitting the button was to try to end a low. The only reason why people drink alcohol is also to try to end a low. Perhaps the low is lack of self-confidence, courage or self-respect. They may drink to help with inhibition, shyness, insecurity, lack of concentration, stress, boredom, deprivation or just plainly and simply to end the low of not being able to enjoy themselves without the drug. The problem is that alcohol causes all of these lows. It never genuinely relieves them or solves them. It is so clear when you look at it with an open mind. The relaxing drinks are the ones taken at relaxing times. The drinks that make you happy are taken at happy times. The drink never changes, only the situations. It is always the situation that is special, never the drink.

Alcohol had destroyed my courage and confidence so subtly over so many years that I wasn't aware of it but all the time I thought it was doing the opposite. I had been conditioned to believe that alcohol helps people to enjoy their lives; that it helps give them courage, helps them relax and gives them confidence. I now see very clearly that they are not particularly happy, relaxed or more confident with alcohol but very miserable, insecure and certainly not relaxed without it. The alcohol itself simply creates all the illusions and, backed up by the massive brainwashing that's gone on, we believe these illusions to be true. It is such a clever confidence trick but that is all it is, a trick, a con.

Look at people who have never drunk alcohol. There aren't many in this country and some of the only examples are children or those with religious constraints. There are some adults who have never had an alcoholic drink who go to parties and enjoy themselves or love a relaxing bath. They have confidence and they have courage. When you drink and are in exactly the same social situation as them, you are never happier or more relaxed than them. Nor do you have more courage or confidence than a non-drinker. The sad reality is that you have a great deal less.

Alcohol suppresses your central nervous system, your courage, confidence and self-respect. So the person who doesn't need to drink wins hands down every time. When they are happy it is true happiness, when they are relaxed it is true relaxation, when they are confident it is true confidence. When you drink it's all false. Why do you feel as though you need alcohol and they don't? It's because of the drug itself and the indoctrination. Alcohol creates fear and insecurity and it is these feelings that keep people hooked on something that they wish they didn't need. It is fear of many things but the worst fear that we have been conditioned to believe is that you can never be truly free from alcohol addiction. But as I will repeat once more, all these fears and insecurities are created by the drug itself and the brainwashing since birth. Once you get rid of all that brainwashing and you purge the poison from your body, all the fears are immediately removed. You never had these fears before you started taking the drug and you won't have them again after you stop; it's only drinkers who have them. I now no longer have these fears. I was having that drink was because of the harmful effects of the last drink. I was the mouse yet I thought I was a 'tru' man!

The advantages of not drinking could fill another book. As I have said, the difference is like living in another world; more money, fitness, health, energy, courage, self-confidence, ability to relax, self-respect, mental and physical vibrancy, happiness, freedom from having to exercise control over my addiction and yes, a better love life. I'm truly free.

This is something organisations like AA believe is not only hard but impossible to achieve. According to them you can stop drinking but, instead of true freedom, the best you can expect is a life in ...

'Recovery'

You may or may not have heard about 'alcoholics' who stop drinking and remain in 'recovery' for the rest of their lives. This, apparently, is one of the symptoms of being an alcoholic. One of the many books I read about alcohol was *The Joy of Being Sober* by Jack Mumey. In it he states quite categorically that you are different to everyone else, that you have inherited your 'disease' from your family and that alcoholism is in your genes. He also states throughout his book that the recovery process is hard, long and, oh yes, it never ends. He tells you this at the very start of the book and, to be honest, I think Mr Mumey should have been done under the Trade Descriptions Act for calling it *The JOY of Being Sober*. It sounds a riot from the start, doesn't it?

Incidentally this isn't the only book that refers to this ongoing 'recovery' period; in fact all the books on alcohol do. In any case, how long does it take to recover fully? Well here's the problem: apparently you never can. You can only expect to achieve a satisfactory way of life, taking each day as it comes, according to leading experts in alcoholism. So why can't we ever recover? It is because there is apparently no cure for this disease. When you confront these 'experts' and ask them what disease they are talking about, they simply say 'alcoholism.' When I ask them to explain what is the cause of the disease, they tell me the answer is not clear but that once you have the disease there is no cure. They go on to say that maybe once we establish the cause we can begin finding a cure. Find the cause? Hellooooo, is there anybody home? What are 'they' talking about? Do you really have to have a BA Honours in common sense to figure out that alcohol is the cause of the disease? If somebody takes heroin regularly or smokes cigarettes, do we say that the answer is not clear? Do we say that we do not know what the cause is? Of course it's clear, it's very clear.

The actual chemical addiction to alcohol is a disease in itself and I agree with that. If you want to call the disease alcoholism, fine, but the disease can only get worse while you are still taking the drug. The disease can also only be there while you are taking the drug. The disease ends the second you stop taking it. The disease *is* the drug. The 'recovery' process takes place all the time when you are drinking alcohol as the body desperately tries to heal itself, not when you aren't. The disease has completely gone the very second you purge it from your mind and body. What is so difficult to understand about that?

They say that you are never really cured but in recovery for the rest of your life. This is because if you have just one drink then it will trigger the 'disease' again. If you cannot be cured in the first place, then you must still have the disease even when you are not drinking, so how can it start again if you have a drink? How can something start again if, apparently, it could never be stopped in the first place? Even the experts' own arguments don't make sense. By their rationale, every person on the planet was born with a disease called 'heroinism.' If you were to start taking heroin, then the chances are you will want to take more and more. It would destroy you mentally and physically and affect every area of your life but, please remember, if the drug takes hold it's not actually the drug that is the problem, it's you. The problem lies in the fact that you were born with this disease called heroinism. Who in their right mind would believe such rubbish? This recovery nonsense has nothing whatsoever to do with people's genetic make-up, character or personality. It is simply mental deprivation because they believe they are missing out on a genuine pleasure or crutch. I hate to simplify it but it really is that simple.

Can you imagine somebody falling into quicksand and afterwards their rescuer saying, 'Now, I am afraid to tell you that you are not truly free. You are now in "recovery" from quicksand which will last for the rest of your life. It is not going to be easy as you will always want to jump back in. You will have a constant battle with yourself every day for the rest of your life but you must understand that you are not able to jump back in because, if you do, you will probably sink and die. You must make a vow to yourself that you are going to stay on firm ground for one day. Just one day and that is today. Take each day as it comes but always remember, once a quicksand sinker always a quicksand sinker.' To which you might reply, 'But that will mean spending the rest of my life wishing I could jump into quicksand with the knowledge that it will destroy me if I do. I feel as if I'm in a no-win situation. Does quicksand do this to everyone who jumps in?' Their answer would be, 'No I am sorry to say, you are the problem, not the quicksand. It is in your genetic make-up – you were born a quicksand sinker.'

Perhaps this sounds a little stupid but then so is the whole business of recovery. Maybe you are thinking, 'Why would you go through the rest of your life wanting to jump back into the quicksand when you know what it is like and have already been pulled free?' That's a very good question but why would you want to inflict a disease on yourself after you have already been cured of that same disease? Why would anybody want to have a disease anyway?

This recovery is nothing more or less than the willpower method of trying to come off any drug. With other drugs it's called willpower; with alcohol it's called recovery. Why? Because we have been so brainwashed and conditioned to believe that the imbibing of alcohol is normal and people who cannot control their intake are not normal. The only logical thing to say is that they have a disease but, as I have illustrated, there is no such thing as a normal drinker and nobody is ever in control; it's just plain drug addiction and drug addiction is a disease in itself. The normal drinker already has the disease, they just don't realise it. The people who realise are labelled alcoholics.

The reason why the willpower method is so difficult is because the person stopping believes they are making a genuine sacrifice. They really believe they are giving up a genuine pleasure or crutch so the second they say 'I am never going to drink again' they feel very psychologically deprived. Think about it logically. Even if the person doesn't drink again but believes they are missing out on a pleasure or crutch, the feeling of deprivation can be there, not just for that day, but for the rest of their lives. It is this and this alone – the waiting, the doubting and the uncertainty – that people call 'recovery.' Is it any wonder that someone who stops drinking after being told they are not normal feels miserable? What a prospect and what a disincentive to being free of your addiction.

When you actually confront the experts about where this recovery takes place and where it hurts, they don't actually know. They will go on about the DTs but even a lot of that is caused by the mental deprivation. Besides, they only last for a few days, if they happen at all, so where is the problem after that? It's purely psychological and is caused only by the feeling of deprivation; no more, no less.

This explains why there are some people who haven't had a drink in years but are still pining for one. In fact, unlike smoking where there are now millions of ex-smokers out there who don't miss cigarettes, with drink, not only does around 80 per cent of the UK population drink the stuff and believe the illusions and brainwashing but the 20 per cent who don't are largely made up of whinging ex-drinkers.

I attended an AA meeting many years ago at which I heard a complete diatribe of sheer gloom, doom and misery. I must stress once more that AA has helped many, many people and not all their meetings are like this. Some can be very entertaining but I also believe that there is no need to go to a building every week, state your name and complain about no longer having to drink. It would be a lot more understandable if they went somewhere every week and shouted at the tops of their voices, 'Isn't it great, I don't have to drink any more!' The first person in this AA meeting stood up and said, 'I am John, I am an alcoholic.' It turned out that he hadn't had a drink in twenty years! Twenty years, yet he still said that there wasn't a day that went by when he didn't miss it. Miss what? There is simply nothing to miss. The pleasure or crutch of alcohol is merely an illusion based on the removal of natural fears and years upon years of advertising, conditioning and brain-washing. Think about this for a moment, twenty long years and probably until the day he dies, that poor man has been and is probably still mourning something he hopes he will never have again. Now that is a ludicrous and intolerable way to go through life, isn't it?

I read Frank Skinner's excellent and, as you'd expect, very funny autobiography. In it were a couple of things that illustrated just how some people are never mentally free from alcohol and remain in a permanent state of recovery. Sometimes he's asked after a performance, 'Were you happy with that?' His reply? 'No I haven't been happy since September 24, 1986.' This was the last time he had an alcoholic drink. I must say I love Frank Skinner. I think he's really funny and sharper than Mr Sharp of Sharpsville (each to their own!) but, after reading that, I felt really sorry for him. He, like so many other members of the 'recovery gang,' is in a no-win situation. Does he spend the rest of his life wishing he could have something which he hopes he will never touch again or does he give in to his own frustration and become the lab mouse once more? What a choice. He has simply opted for what he believes is the lesser of two evils called 'recovery.'

People who stop drinking for a couple of weeks also suffer from this mental deprivation as they have to exercise immense willpower, discipline and control in order to 'give up' for just a short time. Are these people in recovery? After all, they are going through exactly the same thing as the people in AA – mental deprivation. They cannot say it's recovery otherwise they would be seen as an alcoholic and that would mean their having to admit, for the first time, that alcohol is a drug like any other and that they are simply hooked.

I have repeatedly emphasised throughout this book that it's easy to stop drinking and, more importantly, to stay happily stopped for the rest of your life. People only disbelieve this because of the brainwashing, largely perpetuated by other people's attempts to stop or by watching others who have tried to stop by going about it in the wrong way and feeling miserable. This gives the impression that it is difficult or impossible to achieve freedom. There are, after all, whinging ex-drinkers who moan because they have a disease from which they can't be cured. You have seen people off the drink for two weeks telling you every day that they haven't had a drink for x number of days. At the same time they opt out of their normal lives by saying they would love to go out but just can't as they are not drinking. This simply perpetuates the false belief that people cannot enjoy themselves in the same way without a drink.

People, possibly even you, who cannot drink just for one evening because they are driving have been heard saying that the evening was pretty lousy because of it. So you think, 'If it's like that for a day, then what the hell would it be like forever?' If you have been conditioned to believe that you are an alcoholic, then you begin your attempt to stop with the knowledge that you will never be free. Isn't that at the root of the fear that keeps people hooked? The fear is that you will always be missing out so it's no wonder people don't start off with a feeling of excitement, elation and freedom. We have been so brainwashed into believing that we can never get free or that it is not normal to be sober, that we begin our attempt to stop drinking with a sense of doom and gloom, as though we have just made a real sacrifice. Instead of feeling elated, liberated and joyful at the knowledge that we have just freed ourselves from one of the worst slaveries ever, that we have just stopped a progressive disease in its tracks and will never have to suffer again, we are led to believe that it is the end of nothing more than a disease and not the beginning of something great.

Let me ask a question – at what point did Nelson Mandela realise that he was free from his imprisonment? At what point was he free, never to return? Was it a year after he was released from that prison, a few months, a week, a day or was it the very second he was released? It was, of course, the very second he was let out, the very second he stepped outside to freedom. Do you think he ever had a craving to go back in? No, he knew for certain that he was free the moment he stepped out but at what point can the poor ex-drinker say, 'Have you heard the news, I've done it, I'm free. I never have to drink alcohol again, isn't it marvellous!' At what point can they become elated to be free. At what point will the craving go? The answer is never, or at least not while they still believe they are making a sacrifice.

I accept that, in order to free yourself from any disease, you have to accept that you have the disease but it's just as important to realise when you don't have it any more. There is nothing sadder than a person who has freed themselves from a slavery, an addiction or a disease but has no idea that they have. The problem is that society gives you the impression that you have indeed made a genuine sacrifice and that you will be the one missing out. So, when people stop drinking they don't start with a celebration of their freedom from an awful addiction but with a sense of doom and gloom, wondering when they will fail. If the poor drinker believes that he or she can never escape, they never will. Even if they don't drink for the rest of their lives, they will simply be waiting to see whether or not they will fail.

The trauma that ex-drinkers suffer when they stop is not caused by the awful physical pain of the drug leaving the body or by anything in their genes, but by the mental deprivation. It feels like a child being deprived of a toy. Our theory is that if we suffer the misery of this frustration for long enough then, eventually, we might be able to reach the stage where we can say, 'I've done it. I'm free.' However, true freedom is impossible that way. While you still believe you have made a sacrifice the frustration will be there forever as, unless all the brainwashing is removed, the sense of deprivation will always remain. This is not recovery or remission, it is simply mental deprivation which results in a feeling of missing out. Exactly what is there to be deprived of? What does alcohol do for you or anybody for that matter? The answer is absolutely nothing. It's just one massive confidence trick. Once I stopped for three months and whinged constantly. Looking back now, I see that it was all unnecessary as I was moping about something that did not exist.

In order to succeed, it must be clear in your mind that nobody is ever born an alcohol addict, any more than anyone is born a coffee drinker or Mars Bar eater for that matter. There is only one reason why people get hooked on alcohol and that is the brainwashing, or to put it another way ...

The Advertising

There are only two kinds of advertising that get us hooked in the first place, or that keep us hankering for a drink after we have stopped. They are:

1. Direct and commercial advertising

2. Other drinkers

Let's not underestimate the power of advertising. It works, which is why the alcohol industry spends over £200 million every year advertising their drug in the UK alone. Add that to the spend on indirect promotional activities and sponsorship, the total value of these marketing activities probably exceeds £800 million.

If this drug were launched today, nobody would go near it. Alcohol would never be legal, that's for sure. If you believe that you would be drinking alcohol without the influence of advertising and other drinkers, then imagine visiting another country which knows absolutely nothing about alcohol and trying to sell the stuff to them. It would not so much be difficult as damn near impossible.

Today if you tried to sell alcohol to people who have never come across it, you couldn't. It would be virtually impossible as it would just sound too ridiculous. Imagine telling them that they would have to spend quite a lot to buy a liquid that made them confused, silly, rude, argumentative, sick and that they would need more and more of it to alleviate the unpleasant effects of the previous day's drinking. It is extremely unlikely that anyone would choose consciously to take this product which is my point exactly. Nobody is drinking out of choice because, either they have to or they are miserable and cannot cope. That is why the thought of quitting sends people into a panic. But why should it?

At the start of this book I said that I would like you to open your mind, so let me now try to persuade you to take this brand new drug that I have just been handed. Forget about alcohol for a second, this is a new drug. Think about it as though it were something like heroin or crack. First I will give you a complete list of all the disadvantages of taking this drug, then a very comprehensive list of the advantages.

Finally, I will pose a question which I would like you to answer honestly.

First, here are the disadvantages:

- The drug comes in liquid form which is the result of a process of decay.

- It tastes disgusting.

- It is very addictive and the chances are that you will remain hooked for the rest of your life.

- It will cost you at least £100,000 in your lifetime.

- It is a powerful poison.

- Every fix will destroy thousands of your brain cells.

- It will dehydrate your body so much that the day after imbibing it your brain will have shrunk.

- It will dull all your senses.

- It will stupefy you.

- You will not be able to hold normal conversations.

- It will slow down your reactions.

- It will impair your ability to communicate efficiently and effectively.

- It will slur your speech.

- It will remove your natural fears making you vulnerable and completely unprotected.

- It will remove the safety checkpoint between your brain and mouth and you will blurt out whatever comes into your head, no matter how stupid, offensive, obnoxious, aggressive, rude or outrageous it may be.

- It will create the illusion that you are now more confident and more courageous because you will lose your natural protection.

- Once you have experienced that illusion, you will become completely dependent on the drug and will not be able to enjoy yourself without it.

- Your body will quickly build up an immunity and tolerance, so you will need more and more to get the same illusory effect.

- The more you take, the more it drags you down; the more it drags you down, the more you take.

- It will destroy your courage.

- It will undermine your confidence.

- It will take away your self-respect.

- It will make you its slave for life.

- You will reach the stage where it drags you down so much that you end up despising yourself for being a slave to something that you will eventually hate.

- I should also warn you that, the first time you take it, you will probably be physically sick as it is so poisonous the body must get rid of it as quickly as it can, otherwise you could die.

- The drug in itself is a powerful anaesthetic, which means that it will make you fall asleep; if you are lucky that is, but chances are you will want to close your eyes but the room will spin around and make you feel sick, so you will try to keep them open but will be unable to because the drug has made you sleepy.

- When you wake up from your ordeal your head will be pounding and you will have one of the worst headaches you have ever experienced. This is caused by your blood trying to pump through a dehydrated brain.

- Your whole body will feel as if you have just been run over by a truck.

- It will take at least three days for the effects of the drug to wear off.

Those are the disadvantages of taking this new drug. Now for the advantages:

- Nothing at all.

- Absolutely nothing.

- Nil.

- Zero.

- Zilch.

Now ask yourself this. Would you like some of this new drug? How much money would you pay me for it? Be honest here please.

Unfortunately, this wasn't how alcohol was advertised when I was growing up. It isn't today and never will be. Why not? It's because alcohol represents a multi-trillion pound industry worldwide. The bottom line is that they want your money. Alcohol is the last recreational drug that is still allowed to be advertised on television; consequently the manufacturers do it all the time. The majority of sporting events are sponsored by the alcohol giants; there are huge billboards everywhere promoting the drug and you will see glossy magazines with full page ads for alcohol on every other page. The advertisements project images of 'coolness' or being 'one of the lads' drinking beer, of wine sophistication for the ladies or Scotch for the business executive. Just wake up to all this bollocks as it's simply intended to keep you hooked on a drug from which trillions are earned. The government won't stop the advertising either as it's big business for them. Our own government earns billions of pounds a year in revenue from a drug which is known to kill around 9,000 people every year and destroys thousands of lives at the same time.

The advertising even suggests that your love life will be enhanced by alcohol. 'Just add the vodka' said one campaign in which two girls were getting, well, let's say very close. We are also bombarded by images of the 'fine' bottle of wine, open fire, nice music and sweet lovemaking. What a romantic scenario, and the fact is that without the alcohol you would remember everything and feel every touch, sensation and moment. The reality of alcohol is usually anything but that. Alcohol dulls all your senses, so you cannot feel anything anyway. Too much of the stuff and men know all too well what can happen – it isn't called 'brewer's droop' for nothing. The only 'stiff one' you can fix is the drink and sometimes all the scaffolding in the world won't keep it up. The opposite can happen too where your senses are blown so much that you cannot focus on what you are doing; you simply cannot reach a climax no matter how hard you try, so bear that in mind boys!

This book is about reality, not lies and advertising and, although I hate to admit it, I can honestly say that sometimes I couldn't even remember having sex!

At other times I could remember up to a certain point and the next thing I knew, the alarm was going off. My mouth would feel like dirt and my breath stank of alcohol at 8 a.m. How romantic is that? It's funny how they don't advertise that to the kids when they are growing up. I was so trapped that I honestly thought that sex was better after a few drinks. What rubbish. The best sex or lovemaking for men and for women takes place when you are sober, clear-headed and, above all, have all your senses about you. Some people dispute this but it is only because they have drunk alcohol virtually every time they've made love, so have simply forgotten how wonderful it can be when sober. Making love is a happy situation, it is not the drink. Think about it: would you rather make love to a drunk or a person who knows what they are doing? If you know what you are doing, at the very least you won't wake up in the morning wondering who is next to you.

Every television programme, film and even plays portray alcohol as a social pastime, perpetuating the illusion that it gives courage, confidence, relaxation and happiness. The truth behind the drug is never advertised. Even in pubs like the Rovers Return and The Queen Vic where the entire cast of *Corrie* and *EastEnders* seem to live, nobody is drunk. In fact if you were hooked, of all the pubs in the world, these are the ones you would do your utmost to avoid. When someone in these soaps does get drunk, they are seen as alcoholics and told to leave the pub. It is exactly the same in real life. Huge amounts of money are spent advertising alcohol and most pubs and clubs will try to tempt you with 'happy hour' promotions but the minute you get drunk you will be thrown out for taking up those same offers. They sell you a drug which stupefies you, makes you act irrationally, obnoxiously or violently and which compels you to have more and more yet, the minute it takes effect, they want you out of their establishment. What hypocrisy!

Anyway, how do these people in the soaps afford to drink from morning till night? Many of them are unemployed, so the soap pubs must be the cheapest in the world. After all it is a very expensive drug. All this subliminal advertising has a powerful brainwashing effect, whether or not we are aware of it. We see images every day presenting it as normal and natural to drink every lunchtime and evening. We become immune to the fact that it is completely unnatural to destroy our brain cells, courage and confidence on a weekly if not daily basis. Consequently we end up believing that it's normal to drink.

> It is not normal or natural to drink alcohol.

Sport and alcohol now go hand in hand, from beer or lager for football to champagne for tennis. During 'France 98' (the football World Cup) Carling, the main sponsors of UK football at the time, put a St George's Cross on each can during the competition. For the

South Africa World Cup in 2010, they did it again. The association they wanted drinkers to make was England = Carling. Such is the power of advertising that it worked. Also, the major supermarkets advertised three 15-packs of beer at silly prices as low as £18. Imagine the number of comatose fans there must have been in front of their TVs watching the matches.

Drinking alcohol is frequently advertised as rebellious. 'Go to the dark side' one advertising slogan suggests and '94.7 per cent Good' proclaims another. Advertisers always challenge us to be different, to rebel and say 'let's live,' 'I don't care' or 'sod it' to society. Let's get something very clear, there is nothing different or rebellious about doing the same thing as around 80 per cent of the population. If you really want to be a rebel or be different, become a person who doesn't need to take alcohol in order to enjoy or cope with life.

Just look at the way in which alcohol is advertised as refreshing. It is just lie after lie. There is one old ad that showed a world that has run out of water. The sun is blazing and H_2O is the most sought after commodity in this world; so much so that dealing in water is big business in the underworld. The ad shows a hunky man (what else, as they wouldn't feature someone with an enormous beer gut) walking through this world where everyone is dying of thirst. He then goes into a building, climbs the stairs and there is a beautiful woman (of course) pouring him a pint. It ends with the slogan: 'In a world that is losing its head, a lager that doesn't.' The lager might not 'lose its head' but if you drank it, you would. You might not only lose your head but also your family, home, money, brain cells, self-respect, courage, confidence and, as in 9,000 cases in the UK every year, your life. If there were no water in the world, the last thing you would do would be to drink alcohol as it would drain any fluid you did have from your body.

I could go on about all the advertising but there really is no need. You know exactly what I'm talking about. After all, you are bombarded with it every minute of the day; it's everywhere. The message in all these adverts remains the same: 'our job is to keep you hooked and get your money.'

Whether you realise it or not, all the advertising exists to keep you hooked or makes a desperate bid for you to change your brand. They will change the shape of their bottles, their image, even give the same product different names to rebrand and make them look new. No matter how powerful this direct advertising is, it didn't get us hooked in the first place so what on earth persuades us to take this drug at all? Was it really the poster ad for alcohol which made you leap up and order your first drink? No. It was one thing and one thing alone, the same thing that causes everybody to try any drug. It's the people who are already hooked on that drug. In other words, in the case of alcohol, it's ...

Other Drinkers

Every year the alcohol industry spends literally billions worldwide advertising their drug, yet it's their sales force that pays them because alcohol addicts are the biggest sales force the industry has. Even comedian Jack Dee, who said he attended AA has advertised alcohol on television. Keep it clearly in your mind that most drinkers you meet work for the alcohol industry. They have no idea they do, but they do. Just remember this when you stop drinking and break free from this slavery.

Looking back, I know I certainly did. I played my part in recruiting new customers. I once tried very hard to get a friend of mine hooked. She had never drunk alcohol in her life and had no desire whatsoever to do so. However, due to my massive brainwashing, I couldn't understand why she didn't want to drink. Every time we went out I would say, 'Go on, have a drink. What's the matter with you? You really don't know what you are missing.' I would even say, 'What a shame you don't drink.' You see, when you are hooked on a drug it becomes a mystery how anybody can enjoy life without it. The mystery now is how on earth I believed I was enjoying myself when I was hooked.

The sad reality is that other drinkers really do not mind if you stop drinking, provided you are miserable. In fact they might even view it as a game to see just how long you will stay off the alcohol. If you are moping around, getting uptight, depressed and longing for a drink they are fine but if you are happy about stopping, they hate it. This is because drug addicts do not like to be reminded that they need a drug and that, unintentionally, is exactly what you are doing when you enjoy life and cope easily without drink. So be alert as their constant need to justify their intake can lead them to try to get you hooked again. As I have already said, if you stop smoking you are a hero; if you stop drinking you are seen as a freak.

They will say things like, 'How are you finding it?', 'How's it going?', 'It's early days yet' or the classic question, 'Are you still not drinking?' Just so you are more than equipped for this attitude, be aware that you will be asked *that* question until the day you die. I was getting it thrown at me all the time when I stopped. 'Still off the sauce Jace?,' 'How long has it been now then?,' 'How are you finding it?' Finding what? What the hell was I supposed to be looking for? When somebody passes their driving test do you phone them up a week after they have passed and say, 'Can you still drive?' Of course you don't but we have been conditioned for so long to believe that it is impossible to stop drinking and be happy about it for the rest of your life that everybody is simply waiting to see *when* you will give in to temptation.

You can only ever be tempted if you buy into the advertising message that alcohol will provide you with some genuine benefit. If you are truly free you cannot give in to temptation because you cannot be tempted by something that has no appeal. You can only 'give in' to something if you have 'given up' something and that is the best part of stopping drinking. It turns out that, contrary to what we have been made to believe, there is absolutely nothing to give up. The very expression 'I've given up' implies sacrifice which is why people suffer after they stop. They believe they have made a sacrifice by giving up something worth having, which of course is rubbish. They are in fact curing themselves of a progressive disease and stopping an addiction. It is the other drinkers who are publicising it and making the huge sacrifices. They are the ones giving up their health, money, courage, confidence and freedom. Whether they know it or not, they are drug addicts and, as such, have a progressive disease. That is not something to envy, it is something to pity.

The question, 'How are you finding not drinking?' is ridiculous anyway. The real question should be, 'How is the drinking going? How are you finding the hangovers, the memory loss, the cost, the arguments, the lethargy, the slavery, the having to control your intake, etc.? Believe me they will soon drop the subject. You will probably get the inevitable answers like 'I don't get hangovers' which simply means that they have built up such a tolerance to the drug that hangovers have become the norm. Or it may be simply that they are lying like any other drug addict in order to justify their intake.

Most drinkers try to justify why they choose to drink, especially if they are with somebody who has stopped and, even worse, who clearly doesn't miss it and has no need for the drug any more. The alcohol never changes, only the excuses. If you ask a young kid why they are drinking they will say 'I enjoy it.' They are lying and it's obvious to both parties that they are not really enjoying it. Every time they take a sip they shudder, they get very intoxicated and feel like shit the next day. Some even vomit when they first drink alcohol and wish they were having a lemonade instead. The problem is that they have been conditioned to believe that it's not adult to drink lemonade any more, so while in the experimental process of taking alcohol they will say 'I enjoy it.' They are trying to justify their intake from the start and it never stops. If you ask the same youngster why they drink a few weeks later they will now say 'I like the taste.' What they really mean is that they no longer find the taste offensive. Ask them some time later and they will say 'It gives me courage, confidence, helps me to relax and makes me feel happy.' So, in just a few short months, the alcoholic drink has changed from something that made you feel dreadful and tasted awful, into something which not only tastes good but is also a crutch. It's blatantly obvious that the drink itself hasn't changed; merely the youngster's perception of alcohol.

All through our lives our reasons for drinking change from one drink to the next in order to try to justify why we do it but the real reason always remains the same: it's alcohol addiction. So be alert as the majority of drinkers will do this. They will say stupid things which appear to be good and sound logical but which are, in reality, pathetic. They are so scared of stopping that when *you* achieve something that they think is out of their reach, they will try anything to drag you back. You might say things like, 'Have you heard the news? I don't need to drink any more. I'm free.' After all, it is worth saying as it's not every day you free yourself from slavery and stop a disease in its tracks. You will inevitably get more responses like, 'Well how long has it been? I wouldn't speak too soon – it's early days yet.' What the hell has time got to do with it? Does it really matter how long you have been free, just as long as you are free? That is all 'recovery' is; counting the days waiting for something to happen. But waiting for what? The day you can say 'I've done it. I don't need to drink any more. I'm free'? The truth is that you can say it from day one and if you say it from day one then you are truly free from day one. If you do not say it on day one, then when are you going to say it?

There is no need whatsoever to count days when you stop drinking, it's pointless. This is a very important part of the method.

DO NOT COUNT DAYS WHEN YOU ARE FREE.

From the second you know you have consumed your last drink you are free. This is without doubt the most bizarre prison in the world. It is the only prison where people count the days after being released.

Such is the nature of the alcohol confidence trick that drinkers will actually believe that you are missing out and this is precisely why they will be baffled as to why you have stopped drinking altogether. If you were already seen to be an 'alcoholic' in their eyes, they will feel sorry for you because you can't drink any more. What they will not understand is that they are the ones missing out and, once fully understood, you will be feeling sorry for them. It becomes very easy to see that they are deprived and it is they who have to exercise control over a drug on which they are dependent. If you do not consume alcohol you are being deprived of absolutely nothing.

> If you do not consume alcohol you are being deprived of absolutely nothing.

Focus clearly on the reality of the situation. No matter how long you have stopped, it is the poor drinkers who are the ones missing out and ultimately being deprived. They are being deprived of their health, their money, their brain cells, their memory, their senses, their peace of mind, their courage, their confidence and, most of all, their physical and mental freedom. They are the drug addicts and you will be one of the first to truly see them for what they are. I doubt if you would envy a heroin addict so why envy alcohol addicts?

THERE IS NOTHING TO ENVY
AND SO MUCH TO PITY.

Always remember what got us all hooked in the first place. It was the drinkers. It was the drinker who convinced us we were missing out. If I had the job of making somebody believe in Santa Claus, I would recruit a child to do it for me. What better person to convince somebody of an illusion than someone who honestly believes that illusion to be true? Don't forget the drinkers themselves are being deluded as a part of them believes the illusions. Never underestimate the power of other drinkers and the huge amount of brainwashing they pass on. It seems that everyone drinks the stuff, from the down-and-out on the street to the President of the United States.

We have been conditioned from birth to drink alcohol. Even your own parents may have thought there was no harm in your having a little glass of wine with a meal when you were ten. 'What's wrong with a little glass of wine?' is almost the same as saying, 'What's wrong with a little heroin?' They are both drugs, they are both addictive and they both destroy lives. The only difference is that one is seen clearly for what it is and is not being pushed on every TV programme or film as a sociable, stress relieving happy pill whereas the other one is. Remember, the only difference between heroin and alcohol is that one is legal. One is seen for what it actually is and the other is seen from an addict's perspective.

The main problem with alcohol is that, unlike heroin, the addiction is so subtle that many have lived and died without ever realising they were addicts. Unfortunately, even if they had been aware of their dependency, they would have had to block it from their minds for fear they might have an incurable disease and have to turn into a social recluse. You know, that mystery disease known as alcoholism.

Drinkers continue to try to justify their intake with deceit and lies, not only to others but particularly to themselves, just like any drug addict. However, do not let this cloud the issue as, no matter what drinkers believe and regardless of anything they say, the truth is that they are hooked. This is not me being arrogant, it is fact. They may not even realise they are trapped but they are. As such, it means they are suffering from drug addiction and have a disease which, slowly but surely, will get worse and worse. It means they have to exercise control which means they are controlled. Always keep it clear in your mind that drinkers are never in true control. It is a form of self-imposed torture to try to control a drug. Ultimately the drug always controls its victim, dictating to the addict and not the other way around. This is the main reason why they remain hooked or get hooked again as they believe they can control alcohol.

I stopped for three months and one of my reasons for drinking again was that I felt it could do no harm as I could control it. But that was precisely the problem. Why would you want to try to gain control of something that does nothing for you? Why would you want to try to control a disease instead of getting rid of it? Why would you want to spend the rest of your one and only life using willpower and discipline trying to manage a drug that does absolutely nothing for you whatsoever? You would only want to control it if you thought you were missing out on a genuine pleasure, which of course you are not. That is exactly what got us all hooked in the first place. After all, would you envy someone with HIV even if you knew that it might not develop into AIDS for another twenty-five years? You would never envy someone with a disease that will probably lead to an even worse disease. You would only pity them. Above all you must realise that most drinkers are in the alcohol trap whether they realise it or not. They are simply at different stages of this progressive disease, that's all.

People sometimes say to me, 'If they don't know they are hooked and in a trap, then surely it doesn't matter if they drink as ignorance is bliss.' Imagine that you were in that quicksand but didn't understand the nature of quicksand and you even believed that you were having fun playing in it. If I came along and pulled you out without your consent, you would be annoyed and upset that I had spoilt your fun and would immediately want to jump back in. But if I explained the nature of quicksand and pointed out that you were in fact trapped and there was only one direction which was down, with no chance of escape, would you still want to jump back in? Do you think for one second that you would ever go back in there again? Do you think for one moment that you would feel deprived even if, at the time, you thought you were having fun? Would you actually envy other people slowly sinking in the sand, even if they were only up to their waist or would you pity them and try to help them out? Of course you would want to help them but they wouldn't want your help. They would only ask for your help when they began to realise they were trapped and not until then.

Imagine being in a position where you are sinking in quicksand and you finally realise what is happening. You call for help but instead of help you are told that you are different. You are told that 80 per cent of the population is in quicksand too but they are just fine and normal. They are not sinking at all; it is in fact you with the problem. You just can't handle quicksand and if you seek help to get out, you will be made a social outcast forever because you have a disease for which there is no cure. What is more, you will be miserable and depressed for the rest of your life just because you can't do something that everybody else does. If you were aware that you were sinking, you would think twice about seeking help if that's what you thought would happen, and this is what frustrates me so much. I know this is an odd analogy but it is relevant. Alcohol addicts feel too ashamed to seek help because they have been taught that, if they need help, they are different. Alcohol creates fear as it is and the last thing the drinker needs is the additional fear of being made to feel weak and disease ridden for life.

So this point must be clear: never envy other drinkers as there is nothing to envy. Remember that point, no matter how long you have stopped. The facts about drinking alcohol never change, only their relevance to you. Once you purge the poison from your mind and body completely, you see clearly that there is nothing to miss. People go through a mourning process when they stop drinking, rather like mourning the loss of a close friend. The truth is that drinkers are the ones who are missing out. They need your pity.

This is one of the keys to lifelong success. Drinkers are in a trap that, in reality, they would dearly love to escape. I have realised since I stopped drinking that the majority of drinkers actually envy me. Not for any other reason than I am free. They would love to be in a position where they could enjoy and cope with life without their dependency on alcohol. The only thing stopping them is fear; the fear of quitting. These were the same fears that I had for years. Make a point of observing drinkers. Notice how they just won't let the subject lie when they realise that you genuinely do not need or want alcohol any more. Notice how, at the end of an evening, they have gained nothing by drinking. Notice how they are always telling you that they are in control, how little they need to drink and how they are forever trying to justify why they are having that last one. What you must realise is that, no matter what they say, they would love to be like you and free from an awful slavery.

ALL DRUG ADDICTS LIE, EVEN TO THEMSELVES.

When they see that you are happy about the fact that you don't need to drink any more, they will think that you are superhuman. The fact is that you feel super-human yourself. After all, they would expect you to complain, at least a little. It is only whinging ex-drinkers that perpetuate the illusion that it is a lifelong struggle and a disease from which it is impossible to truly free yourself.

So do not envy drinkers but realise the truth and they will envy you. This is not a trick but a factual way of looking at it. Most drinkers you meet will secretly envy you. I say secretly because they won't admit they do, otherwise it will immediately confirm that they are not in control. So they have to keep up the pretence for as long as possible and say over and over again, 'I'm in control. I don't have a problem.' They say it so much that they start to believe it. Remember, true control is when you no longer have to exercise control.

No drug addict likes taking their drug alone. When I say alone I do not mean by themselves, I mean when they are with others who are not taking the drug. This is when they sense that they are really alone, hence the question, 'Are you going to join me?' They will say any-thing to get you to have a drink, anything to make you join them once again, anything to get you hooked. They will never see it that way as most have no idea they are hooked themselves but they will, whether consciously or unconsciously, be trying to sell you the drug. Not that they are malicious people who want to inflict a disease on you but because they actually believe the illusion and have no idea that it is a disease.

Drinkers get people hooked, get that clear. What better person is there to sell you an illusion than the person who believes it is real? This is the saddest thing about this addiction; people honestly think that they are deriving some genuine pleasure from alcohol and that they are in full control. They don't drink in the morning but they have been taught to believe that it's perfectly normal to drink at any other time.

IT IS NOT NORMAL TO INFLICT A DISEASE ON YOURSELF.

I have already shown that you can never be in control of a drug and that the natural tendency of any drug user is to take more and more, so how come there seem to be so many people who can ...

Take It or Leave It

This is the cleverest part of the trap. This is what really confuses everyone. If it's the same trap for everyone then why don't we all sink at the same rate? Why can some people take it or leave it and others can't? This is without doubt the biggest illusion of all when it comes to alcohol, the mass delusion that people can take it or leave it. This is why there is a divide with this drug: normal vs. alcoholic. The truth is that the natural tendency is to take more and more of the drug, to keep on hitting the button like the mouse in the cage. However, unlike the mouse, we do have a higher consciousness and there is one main reason why some people do not increase their intake and become what society describes as an alcoholic and that is restrictions.

Think about it. The only reason why people do not drink more and more is because they are forced not to drink, either by themselves or society. It is only restrictions which prevent people from becoming what are described as alcoholics any sooner. There are so many restrictions when you think about it, whether it's money, health, effects on the family, because you are driving, because you have to work, fear you will be judged by others, fear you'll turn into an alcoholic, your children, social stigma, being physically incapable of coping with the poison or because you actually hate being drunk.

Money plays a major role in restricting people's intake. After all it is a very expensive drug. Some people simply do not have enough money to increase their intake so they will try to gear it to what's in their pocket. After all, they are already going to spend £100,000 on the drug as it is. It seems funny that the whole thing comes full circle with people at the entrance to the trap drinking cheap alcohol like cider and people at the end drinking cheap alcoholic drinks like cider. I reached the stage where I was drinking Tennants Super and Carlsberg Special Brew. Did I really think they were superior brands or was I simply trying to get more alcohol for less money? This is why people go from beer to spirits; to get more alcohol for less money as, like all drugs, your body builds up an immunity so you need more and more to get the same effect. To get the extra in, it becomes easier and cheaper overall to drink spirits. The fact is that many people cannot afford to increase their intake so they have no choice but to hold it at some kind of level. Even this goes out of the window the further into the trap you get and you reach the stage where you will do without food, family and friends to get alcohol.

Health is another major restriction. Whether drinkers like it or not, the same drug that they think gives them pleasure also just happens to be the number two killer drug in Western society. Just because it's not really talked about doesn't change the reality. I used to have to watch my drinking because of my weight and my unattractive beer gut. Alcohol really does 'weigh' you down in every way.

Looking back now and seeing my drinking from an outsider's perspective, I realise I had to exercise willpower and discipline to some degree every day. This discipline was forced on me most of the time but the confidence trick was so subtle that I thought I was choosing not to drink, not that I simply couldn't. There were just so many restrictions preventing me from drinking more and more. When I had no job and was living in a squat in south London, I drank as much as my pocket would allow. When I had a job, I drank as much as my work would allow. When I was in a relationship, I drank as much as the relationship would allow and so it went on. Isn't this true? Do you find that, sometimes, you simply cannot drink even when you want to? Do you find that if you haven't got to work or are on holiday or not driving that you drink a lot more than when you have to restrict yourself? If you are honest you know that you do. Most drinkers do. If you don't, the chances are you are already on skid row which would mean that you still have to discipline yourself anyway because of the cost.

If alcohol really did all the things that we believed, wouldn't we have more courage, confidence and happiness first thing in the morning? Why delay happiness and have it as soon as we wake up? The reality is that, instinctively, we know that it's all lies. If you drank in the morning you would have no life and would not even experience the illusion of enjoyment. You would feel miserable when you were drinking and miserable when you weren't.

Many smokers have a cigarette first thing in the morning and still function. It is not seen as abnormal for them to smoke in the morning. Alcohol, however, is mind altering so you have to discipline yourself. Many addicts won't even go out some nights because they have to work the next morning. Some addicts will go all week without a drink because of restrictions, whether it's work, their children, having to drive, worry about their health, their money, their business or whatever. They have no choice but to abstain and many simply accept it and crack on with their lives. They are perfectly happy to do so, proving that the physical withdrawal is not the problem. However, as soon as the weekend comes and the restrictions are removed, they take the drug like there is no tomorrow and, having spent all week looking forward to the time when they can indulge, they lose the very weekend they were looking forward to because of that very drug. I know, because I used to do just that.

How many people do you know who say they only drink 'every now and then' but go mad either on holiday or at weekends? Holidays are the time when you see drinkers in their true light. Many drinkers who wouldn't normally touch a drop during the day because of restrictions, often judging others who do, can be seen having a pint on the beach at ten in the morning. That is if they are up that early as, chances are, they won't arrive on the beach until 1 o'clock because they were so plastered the night before. Of course it's OK to drink at 1 p.m., it is perfectly normal, but what they fail to realise is that they have only been up for an hour. But what the hell does time matter anyway? If you drink you drink. Do you think that you would look at a heroin addict differently if they said, 'It's OK, I don't have my first "hit" until 1 p.m., I don't need it first thing'? Of course you wouldn't.

All drug addicts have to exercise control to some degree because of restrictions. The real slavery is this constant need to control and the biggest gain you will get from being totally free is literally that, your freedom. If you are being controlled in any way, then you are not free. If you are dependent on any substance, then you are not free. If you have to look at your watch to see if you can have a drink, then you are not free. If you have to hold it at a certain level because of restrictions, then you are not free. If you are timing your drinks, then you are not free. All drug addicts lie, including drinkers who say things like 'I only have one glass a day.' What they fail to tell you is that it's a pint of Scotch.

There are only two reasons why people do not become heavy drinkers:

1. They are not physically strong enough to cope with that amount of poison at one sitting.

2. They have more restrictions in their lives that prevent the natural increase.

The majority of drinkers can turn into heavy drinkers in an instant. It only takes one really bad moment in life and, wham, they no longer have the strength or the inclination to control their intake and the floodgates open.

Yes but what about ...

Binge Drinkers

Ah yes, binge drinkers. They are the ones who cost the nation £2.7 billion and have led to the UK being dubbed 'Binge Britain.' However, I am not talking about those who just binge at weekends because of the many mid-week restrictions that prevent them drinking. The fact is most of these drinkers triple their intake at weekends. No, I am talking about the group of people who give the impression that they can take it or leave it; I'm talking about those who do not touch a drop for months, then go on a binge. This group usually falls into two distinct categories:

1. Those who really do not think that alcohol has any benefit and do not miss it when they are not drinking.

2. Those who really do miss alcohol when they are not drinking and are, in a sense, simply 'on the wagon.'

In both cases when they drink, they really are drinking. All the restrictions in the world would not stop them. From morning till night they have to drink and there are no half measures. They just continue to hit the button and sod the consequences.

The first category of people who, when they are not drinking, genuinely do not miss alcohol at all can actually see it for what it is when they are off the booze and wouldn't drink the stuff. The problem is, they do believe one of the illusions and that is that it helps to alleviate stress. They binge drink as a way to escape reality when reality has simply become too much and they cannot take it any longer. So it's either join the Foreign Legion or go on a binge. If heroin were legal they would probably use that to blot out life. In a sense it has nothing to do with alcohol addiction; it could be anything that does the job but they choose alcohol because it does not require a prescription, is legal and readily available from almost anywhere. These people are not actually addicted to alcohol and they do not think that there is any pleasure to be gained from drink; they simply think it will act as a catalyst to escapism. The problem is that, because alcohol is a depressant, it actually drags them down even further, giving them more reason to want to escape. They wake up feeling worse than the day before, so they drink even more. The initial reason for wanting to blot out their problems (or get 'blotto') is getting worse by the day because they haven't dealt with the issue, which causes an even greater need for the anaesthetic.

Many binge drinkers have destroyed everything they have worked for in a matter of weeks. One day they realise that drinking is destroying their lives even more than the reason they resorted to it in the first place. Reality dawns and they know that it simply has to stop, so they decide to get on with their lives and quit drinking. These people are playing a dangerous game and if they believe it has one benefit, it won't take long before they believe all the illusions. The time they spend not drinking will decrease and the time they spend bingeing will increase. This type of drinker is rare but does exist, which is why I have covered it here.

The second type of binge drinker is the most common. This is the 'three months on, three months off' drinker. When they are not drinking they are missing it and feel miserable and deprived. However they do not admit to anyone that they feel deprived, and openly judge everybody else who drinks, becoming real 'holier than thou' ex-drinkers, and there is nothing worse. They are resisting the urge to drink all the time, using discipline whenever they are not drinking. Their thoughts are entirely taken up with the effort. Eventually something happens in their life and, as their resistance runs low, they do not have the mental strength to resist any longer.

They have now reached the 'dam' position. This happens when there is so much pressure on the dam from the build-up of water that it starts to crumble causing a deluge. Although the dam appeared strong, it collapses within seconds. It is the same for the poor binge drinker because, in order not to drink, they need to use incredible self-control on a massive scale. Every day the pressure builds up and it simply takes one moment of stress or a big social gathering and, wham, the resolve collapses. Subconsciously they make up for lost time. Their need for the drug is caused by the drug, so the more they have initially, the more they will need the next day. When they are drinking they hate it and when they are not drinking they hate it. During the time spent not drinking they are simply on the wagon and if you are on the wagon it means that you are not drinking for a period of time, therefore it is inevitable you will come off it again.

The problem is that the poor drinker honestly believes that they have fallen off the wagon and to them, the only way to solve this problem is to go back on the wagon. It is not a great deal of fun either, so eventually, it becomes easier to keep drinking even though that's painful too.

Whether binge drinkers are off the drink or on the wagon, they also become 'holier than thou' ex-drinkers. These are the sort of people who do something for years, stop, then spend all their time judging people who do what they once did. The judgemental types also fall into two categories:

1. The drinker who has stopped but is using willpower, discipline and permanent self-control not to drink. These people are the 'recovery mob' who are still missing it and believe they have made a genuine sacrifice. However they do not wish to say this because they would appear weak-willed, so they opt for the 'holier than thou' approach.

2. The person who has never drunk alcohol. When I say never, I mean those who had their first drink and hated it so much that they were just not willing to go through the process of becoming accustomed to it. After all, it's not easy to get over

the foul taste and awful effects that the first drink produces. Virtually everybody has tried alcohol at least once in their lives. These are non-drinkers. They have never been hooked because they have never suffered any of the illusions that the drug creates. These people plainly and simply cannot see why anybody drinks and, because of this, can appear on the surface to be somewhat self-righteous. However, their attitude is more than understandable and is exactly the same as your attitude to people who take heroin. If they knew how desperately heroin addicts wanted to stop, they wouldn't be so quick to judge them either.

What is so wonderful about this method of stopping drinking is that you will not turn into a 'holier than thou' ex-drinker. Once you fully understand the alcohol trap (as you will by the time you finish this book), you will feel genuinely sorry for those who still have to drink and are gradually sinking further and further into the quagmire. You certainly will not be judgemental as you will never forget that you were once there yourself.

I have said that it is only fear that keeps people hooked and so powerful are these fears that the very thought of stopping altogether is just too much. Drinkers think that it will be easier to just ...

Cut Down

No, no, no, no, no! Have I repeated that enough? Cutting down is what alcohol addicts do every day of their lives. As I have just explained, drinkers have permanently to use willpower, discipline and control in order not to increase their intake.

Let me ask you a question: does dieting make food less precious or a thousand times more so? When I was drinking it was like being on an alcohol diet most of the time. When you are on a food diet you have to exercise control and when you are dependent on alcohol you have to do the same. So I was either on an alcohol diet or forgetting the diet and bingeing because I just couldn't be bothered to take control any more.

You have been trying to cut down all your life and that is what this nonsense of going on the wagon is all about. When you made a conscious decision to cut down in the past, did you enjoy the process? Did you have fun being on the wagon or were all your thoughts focused on your next drink? What a way to wish a life away.

This brings me back to Drinkline and their amazing and effective strategies to help reduce your drinking which go something like this.

1.   *Change your routine. Perhaps start drinking later each time, or go out later than usual.*

     I am writing this in disbelief. I have read the
     first strategy on offer to help people reduce their

drinking a few times now but just cannot credit the statement. Start drinking later? Go out later? Is this meant to be real or constructive advice? When I was drinking and arrived at the pub late, my goal was to order as many drinks as I could before the publican called 'time.' Several times I remember waiting to go to the pub but having to wait for others to get ready. I would be very frustrated and pace up and down looking at my watch every five minutes. It was simply because I knew we were missing valuable drinking time. If you have ever arrived in a pub late, do you drink less or do you simply line up more drinks for fear that the 'time' bell could strike at any moment?

2.   *Give yourself time between drinks and set a goal of one drink per hour.*

Do we really need this advice in writing? This is what cutting down is all about and what drinkers do most of the time anyway. As for this business of setting yourself a goal of one drink per hour, have they no idea how alcohol works? Have they ever drunk alcohol themselves? After your second drink, once you have acquired the taste, your conscious mind has been altered and you are in no position to stick to your one drink per hour regime. You simply say 'sod this for a game of soldiers.' The chances are there will be many times when you go out and have just one an hour but who times this? The very second you say that you can only have one drink an hour then you start timing and the drink becomes forbidden fruit once again. This makes it not less precious but more so. The more you tell yourself you can't have, the more you will want. In this situation you will be miserable trying to maintain control and feeling guilty and weak when you fail to achieve.

3. *Do something while you drink such as play darts, bingo or dance.*

    This is the same advice they give for stopping altogether. It really amazes me that people can offer advice like this and are seen as leading experts in their field. What rubbish. Go and play bingo … That's right, go and have a game of bingo, that will help you cut down on your drinking won't it? The last suggestion is the most pathetic by far. Dance? How the hell is dancing going to reduce your alcohol intake? When you dance you get hot and thirsty so you have a drink; drink which will not quench your thirst but cause you to feel dehydrated. So, when you dance again you will be even thirstier. They advise you to do this while you are drinking. Dance while drinking? And don't forget the darts players' bellies.

4. *Try low alcohol and non-alcohol drinks. You may like them.*

    Well, cover me in eggs and flour and bake me for thirty minutes, why didn't I think of that? In fact why didn't we all think of that? All we had to do was drink non-alcoholic drinks. Like them? Why would you when there's real alcohol to be had?

5. *Have something to eat before you start drinking or at least drink some milk.*

Does this make any sense at all? How on earth is this pathetic piece of advice ever going to help you reduce your alcohol intake? After you eat something or line your stomach with milk, it doesn't stop you drinking does it? No, quite the opposite in fact. The alcohol takes longer to reach the brain so you will feel as though you can drink as much as you like. The reality is that you drink more. I used to drink milk before going out sometimes so that I *could* drink more.

6. *Have some days off from drinking.*

Isn't this why we are asking for their advice? We want to know how to do it and still feel happy.

7. *Keep a drink diary and record when you drank, how much you drank and what was the situation leading to your decision to drink.*

Do I even need to say a word on this one? Keep a drink diary? No chance. I would either have been too drunk to remember how many I'd had, why, what the situation was leading to the decision to drink or far too hungover to care anyway. I ask you, do you think these people were actually sober when they wrote this?

8. *Sip your drink rather than gulp it down and put your glass down between sips.*

   So sipping your drink rather than gulping it will help reduce your drinking? No, really? But just how do you stop gulping it down? That is the real question. That is why people are asking for your advice, not so that you will state the obvious.

9. *If you are going to drink, stick to one session of drinking during the day.*

   So if you drink in the morning don't stop all day.

10. *Reward yourself.*

   OK, let's have a drink ... (Oh shit, wrong reward!) It's no good advising a drinker to reward themselves when they still believe that alcohol is reward in itself.

The whole business of giving advice on reducing your intake is ridiculous anyway. This is because alcohol is a drug and you cannot control a drug because if you try, the need will be greater.

Think about it. If you are one of those drinkers who perhaps has a couple in the evening and a skinful at weekends, then in the past you have probably gone for days or weeks without a drink and haven't been bothered by it but, the very second you tell yourself you can't, you have the 'forbidden fruit' syndrome. The reality is that, on the whole, drinkers are strong willed and hate being told what to do by anybody else, including themselves. So when you say they can't drink, alcohol becomes a thousand times more desirable and immediately they feel miserable and deprived, even if they would normally find it easy enough to abstain for a few days. The reason you now find it difficult is because you have told yourself that you can't.

Get this very clear in your mind. When you stop drinking you can drink whenever you wish, just as I can whenever I wish. The difference is that I just don't have any desire ever to drink again. You can, after all, take heroin whenever you wish. Nobody is stopping you, so why don't you? It's because you don't want to, that's why. You can do whatever you want. The choice is yours. You no longer have a choice if you do have a drink as alcohol removes your freedom of choice. All drugs do. You must understand that alcohol is not a hobby or a habit and it is certainly not a genuine pleasure. It is drug addiction; nothing more, nothing less.

Remember that the addiction is only psychological so if you tell yourself that you can't drink you will feel deprived and miserable. The real question should be, 'I can have a drink but what on earth would be the point? What would it do for me?' The answer will be crystal clear – nothing. There is just no point to drinking. Just saying the word 'can't' or believing that you can't would be the only thing that could make it remotely difficult for you to stop drinking or remain free. Remember CAN'T simply means Constant And Never-ending Torture so why put yourself through that?

Trying to reduce your intake simply means not allowing yourself to drink when you want to and having consciously to exercise even more control than before. The longer you suffer any aggravation, the more attractive it will appear when you eventually drink again. If you are banging your head against a brick wall, the longer you do it, the more pleasure you will get when you stop. But it's not pleasure; it's simply the end of an aggravation. Why bang your head against the wall in the first place? Why drink? Why be miserable if you are not drinking? By cutting down you do not stop the drinking but consolidate the idea that alcohol is even more precious than you already thought. That makes you even more hooked than you were as the hook is mental, not physical.

A while ago, radio and TV presenter Chris Evans talked about alcohol on his old morning radio show which was not unusual as he seemed to be obsessed with the stuff. The reality is that he was so hooked that there was not one show I listened to when he didn't mention the drug at least once. On one occasion he was talking about a new book called something like *How to Drink Without Getting Drunk*. According to the book, the way to avoid getting drunk at a dinner party was this: when you first want a sip of wine, don't. Just bring the glass to your mouth and, instead of taking a sip, you should 'nose it.' The next time you want a drink, take a sip of water instead of the wine and only the third time should you actually take a sip. After that you repeat the whole process over again. By doing this you can apparently drink without getting drunk. Oh, what fun. This is cutting down on a supreme level, an intolerable level, a pathetic level as, not only are you thinking about not drinking, you have to be engaged with a routine that ensures you don't forget about it for a moment. What worries me is that the people who give this sort of advice are taken seriously.

Let's get one thing clear. Cutting down is not in any way a stepping stone to quitting. Like everything else when it comes to alcohol, it does the complete opposite. We are dealing with a drug that cannot be controlled and that is why, in order to remain free for ever, we should never fall for ...

'OK, Just the One'

This is, without doubt, one of the most important chapters in the book. To ensure that you have lifelong success, you should clearly understand that there is no such thing as just one drink.

What got us all hooked in the first place? It was the thought of trying just one that got us started. This is where most people who stop drinking make a big mistake. They believe there is no such thing as just one drink which is what makes them feel deprived. The reality is that there is no such thing as just one drink for anybody. The reason for this has nothing whatsoever to do with your genetic make-up, character or personality; it is because alcohol is a drug and, as such, it plays with your mind. If you believe that you will benefit from one drink then you will also think that there must be benefit in a million. There is no such thing as the 'just one' fix of heroin for you either. Why is that? Is it because of your personality or due to your genetic make-up? Is it the nature of the drug? Again, you really don't need to be Sherlock Holmes to work it out.

Sometimes drinkers say to me, 'What's wrong with you, you mean to say you can't have just one?' I reply honestly, 'Yes of course I can, but I don't want to.' I could always turn the tables and say, 'What's wrong with you, you mean to say *you* can't have just one?' After all, there is no such thing as one drink for anyone, especially drinkers. I would never do that as I know there is nothing wrong with them. It is the drug that is the problem.

This point must be made very clear. Drinking starts a chain reaction that will last for the rest of your life unless you break it. It is a disease which gets progressively worse, unless you cure it. Cured means making absolutely certain that, whatever happens, you never have 'just the one.' Make sure that you never, ever re-create the disease because the reason why you will be hooked immediately with just one drink is not because alcohol is physically addictive. If it were, you would be hooked simply after having a piece of chicken in white wine sauce. It is not because the physical withdrawal from that one drink is so awful; it is because, if you view just one drink with genuine pleasure, you will see genuine pleasure in thousands.

About seven or eight months after gaining my freedom I was in a bar while on holiday. I had a glass of sparkling mineral water and my friend had a glass of wine. We were playing pool and, as she was taking her shot, I picked up what I thought was my water but was in fact her wine. It tasted disgusting just like that very first drink. So why didn't I get hooked again although I had taken a gulp of her wine? It is because there was not one part of me that actually wanted to. It was just a simple mistake and at no time did I ever want it. In fact, I couldn't actually believe just how revolting it tasted after all that time. Even though it tasted awful, if I had thought for one second that I would get some kind of pleasure from it, I would have been hooked again. Taste has nothing to do with it as your first drink is disgusting but did that stop you drinking? Of course it didn't. We are dealing with a drug addiction here, so wake up and see it for what it is, not just for now but for the rest of your life. So whenever you think about alcohol, see it for what it actually is and don't respond to the advertising and brainwashing funded by billions of pounds from the industry. It's time to regain control and advertise the reality in your own mind.

Alcohol does nothing for you, so the only time you would even contemplate having just the one is if you thought you were missing out on a genuine pleasure. If I have to repeat this point a million times and scream it from the rooftops I will. When you stop drinking you are giving up absolutely ...

NOTHING!

Oh sorry, apart from the headaches, the hangovers, the lethargy, the bad breath, the beer gut, the arguments, the violence, being overemotional, regretting things you have done but can't remember doing, getting things out of proportion, putting things off all the time, the stress, the overdraft, the taxis, the guilt, the lies, the deceit, the brewer's droop, the mood swings, the breakdown of the immune system, the lack of resistance to all kinds of diseases, the destruction of brain cells, not to mention the excess weight. Oh, I nearly forgot, what you will be giving up most of all is ...

THE DAILY MENTAL AND PHYSICAL SLAVERY
OF BEING A DRUG ADDICT.

What you would be giving up is one of the worst diseases you will ever suffer from, being controlled and dictated to by a drug, frequently not being yourself and, last but by no means least, giving up kebabs. After all, you would never eat them sober, would you?

So now you can see that there is nothing to give up and you will feel no sense of sacrifice whatsoever. If you believe that now, why would you ever get uptight or miserable without alcohol and what power on earth could ever get you to convince yourself that you need just that one more? The answer is the brainwashing that got you hooked in the first place. In order to have lifelong success and to ensure you are never fooled into having the one, you need to understand about ...

Curiosity vs. Craving

If you want not only to stop drinking but also to make sure you remain alcohol free, please make sure you are wide awake when you read this chapter. Knowing the difference between curiosity and craving is perhaps the most important aspect of staying free.

Before we started drinking alcohol we didn't need it. Then the conditioning crept in slowly but surely until we felt as though something was lacking. Our friends were trying it, our parents did it and our role models were drinking, so we thought we were missing out. We weren't sure what it was but we became curious and wanted to try some. This would not have been as a result of an overwhelming craving as, if we had been told at this point that there would be no alcohol at the next party, it wouldn't have bothered us. We did not drink and hadn't yet created a craving for it or a fear that life would not be enjoyable without alcohol. The craving only begins when you think you are missing out on a genuine pleasure.

I wanted a drink before I even started drinking, that is why I had one. It was not because I was a drinker as I had never had a drink in my life and it had nothing to do with any alcohol circulating in my body. My desire was simply due to the massive brainwashing that I had always experienced which made me curious about trying it.

The conditioning is still out there when you stop but the big difference will be that you will know it's all rubbish. You are one of the few people who will see it for what it actually is, which will give you a sense of uniqueness, self-confidence and joy. After finishing this book, you will be better prepared than the few who have never been hooked. The trap is out there and anyone can fall into it at any time. Even people who have never drunk believe that alcohol relieves stress and makes people happy. They believe some of the brainwashing but take the attitude: 'What I've never had I won't miss and I don't want the bad side, thank you.' You should now realise that alcohol does nothing, not just for you but for anybody. The drug will never change, only your perception can change, which is why it is so important to understand what got you hooked in the first place. That way, you can easily avoid it in the future. The aim of this book is not just to help you stop drinking easily but to show you just how easy it is to remain free for the rest of your life.

I was curious enough to want to try the drug ecstasy in the eighties. Everyone was doing it, or so it seemed. The people taking the drug were always trying to sell it. I don't mean sell it for financial gain but sell the effects of the drug. Now I am relieved that I never fell into that trap. I never took the drug but I did come close and this was out of curiosity not craving. There is a big difference. A craving is nothing more than an overriding desire for something. In other words, if you always see alcohol for what it is and not as other drinkers or the alcohol industry want you to see it, then you will never crave it again. You can't crave disease and slavery. As I have mentioned, I never took ecstasy but I had the choice, just as you have the choice of taking heroin if you wish. Had I tried it and the illusory effects of the drug had compounded the brainwashing, the curiosity would have turned into craving. I would have been hooked right then and my freedom of choice would also have evaporated. There are many people who feel they cannot go out without taking one, two, three or more ecstasy tablets. Can you imagine being so dependent on a drug that you feel you cannot enjoy yourself without it? As a drinker you do precisely that.

To ensure your total freedom for life, you must understand that you may be curious again. This curiosity is not there because you used to drink. It is not a craving, nor is it a genuine desire to drink; it is simply an 'action signal.' It is telling you to take action, to retune yourself. It is a signal to remind yourself of the nature of brainwashing and just how powerful it can be so you remember how wonderful it is to be free from the slavery of drug addiction and go on rejoicing in your freedom for the rest of your life. After you are totally free and have been for a while, you sometimes forget all about drinking so it is good to have these occasional moments to remind you of your freedom so you can retune and see alcohol addicts as they are.

All the time our bodies are being polluted by traffic, dust, dirt, chemicals in what we eat and many other external sources. The body, being the ultimate survival machine, will do everything in its power to rid itself of these pollutants to improve the quality and length of your life. Our minds are also polluted and it is our job to rid ourselves of those toxins too. The alcohol industry is a drug industry that has no morals and does not give a hoot about the quality of our lives. Like all drug pushers they are out to make money and will use any method possible to make people dependent on their drug. They know that if you hit their button a few times, you will become dependent.

The industry loses over a million customers a year worldwide and those are just the ones who die so they have to recruit as many new ones as possible. The first fix of any drug is free which is why they will often sponsor student bashes. The people handing out free bottles of beer are young and in their prime. They deliberately choose people who look great to sell their drug, not someone who has just had their leg removed because of bad circulation because of their fix. They do not choose an overweight middle aged man with puffy, red cheeks and an inflated, veined nose, who has lost family, house and job because of alcohol. You can sell an illusion and image but not the reality. You will soon find that, just as your body automatically rids itself of pollutants, your mind will automatically filter any brainwashing that tries to creep back in.

When you stop drinking, the facts will never change but their relevance to you changes completely because you have stopped. You don't worry about your health any longer because you feel a thousand times better. You are not concerned about the money you were spending on the drug and you aren't worried about being a slave to or being controlled by something. In other words you forget why you stopped in the first place, how bad you felt and you forget the truth that lies behind the drug. This is when you should remind yourself of the truth, feel glad because you know what is behind the confidence trick and realise that the drinkers are the ones missing out.

Will this pose any problem? Is this simply a way to fight a genuine desire to drink? Will this happen all the time? Is this just like 'recovery'? No, far from it. In reality, these moments go as quickly as they come, if they come at all. This is not a genuine desire to drink at all. To be honest, I am only putting this in the book to make certain you understand the trap fully so, should anything like that arise, you don't question it or worry about it. You will simply recognise it as a reality check or action signal and once again rejoice in your freedom from that drug.

There are people in really bad relationships, some of whom have been physically and mentally abused for years, and are locked in that relationship through fear. One day they reach the end of their tether and finally pluck up the courage to break free. Once free they might feel a slight emptiness or feel lonely one evening and make the big mistake of forgetting what life was really like by reminiscing about the good times. They then pick up the phone to their ex and, wham, they are back exactly where they started. They can see clearly they are trapped again but now find it even harder to get out. With alcohol, you should remember that there were never any good times. You were happy because of the company, the dancing, the party, the holiday, Christmas or the fact that it was your birthday, not because you were drinking. It was one big illusion designed to keep you trapped.

If you are bored one day it doesn't mean you are low on alcohol. If you do get stressed about something after you stop, the cause of this problem is not an alcohol deficiency. Life is not always a bed of roses whether or not you drink but, because you will be physically and mentally so much stronger, the highs will be much higher and the lows will be nowhere near as low as they were before you stopped.

By this stage in the book you should clearly see that there is absolutely nothing to give up and that you are making no sacrifice at all by quitting alcohol. You now know that the craving was purely psychological and never physical. You also realise that it is the poor drinker who will be deprived and missing out, not you. You know for certain that all traces of alcohol leave the body within three to ten days and, if you have really opened your mind, you will realise that there is no such thing as an alcoholic and that each drinker is hooked like everybody else. Now that you know all this, when exactly is the best time to finally call ...

'Time Please, Ladies and Gentlemen'

So when exactly is the best time to call 'Time please' to put an end to this addiction once and for all? When is the best time to free yourself of a slow and progressive disease? Just when is it right to stop?

RIGHT NOW.

As people's lives slowly deteriorate because of the effects of alcohol, they react by taking more. Those around them try to persuade them to stop and tell them they are out of control which makes them feel even more insecure. So what do they turn to? When will it stop? The answer is 'never' if nobody points out what is really happening. It can and will just get worse and worse and worse.

It is only fear that keeps people hooked.

You have already made up your mind that you are not going to spend the rest of your life as a drinker, so at some point you are going to stop whether you find it easy or difficult. It is only fear that keeps people hooked so don't allow this false fear to keep you imprisoned for the rest of your life. That is exactly what these fears are anyway. The nature of the drug is to fool you. Your problem was that you genuinely thought alcohol gave you some kind of genuine pleasure or a crutch and your fear was not being able to enjoy life or cope without it. The reason you thought this is because you had evidence to back up your fears. Even going on the wagon gave you the evidence to support your fear that you would be miserable without a drink but the fears you have are all false. They only appear real because of past attempts to stop or cut down. These fears will not recreate themselves because they were only a result of failing to understand the nature of the disease and suffering from the CAN'T syndrome (Constant And Never-ending Torture). In other words, the fears created by alcohol mean,

FALSE EVIDENCE THAT APPEARS REAL.

That is to say that the FEAR people have of stopping drinking Appears Real because of the illusory effects of alcohol giving you False Evidence.

Going back to the wonderful *Wizard of Oz*, if you recall, the evil wizard never actually existed. In reality, the scary booming voice which created such incredible fears for Dorothy, the Tin Man, the Scarecrow and the Lion was completely false. Because they couldn't see the reality, the false impression that the voice must belong to something that could destroy them appeared real and created a false fear which prevented them from moving forward and finding their true selves. Yet all it took for their fears to be removed was to see the truth. They push a button which opens some curtains to reveal a little old man speaking into a microphone and moving some machinery in order to create that illusion. Once they see this, there is just no way that the voice could ever create the fear in them again and the minute they know there is nothing to fear, they move forward.

Just like the Wizard, there has never been anything to fear. The truth is that there is nothing at all to fear by stopping drinking and everything to fear by continuing. So what is the best time to get free from any disease or mental and physical slavery? What is really the best time to quit alcohol? The answer is obvious.

ASAP.

It's similar to taking your driving test. You feel nervous for sure but once you have passed, you are euphoric. At what point does the drinker know they are free? It's the very second they see it for what it is, finish their final drink and say, 'That's it. It's over, it's finished. I am now free.' If they do this they are not in remission or recovery, they really are free.

The beauty of being free is that you don't need to wait for anything to happen, because nothing is going to happen. It is the waiting that creates doubts and fears. Once you have decided never to drink again then that's it; it is over from that point and you can jump for joy.

The key to lifelong success is to make the decision, not to hope or think 'would,' 'should' or 'could' but know for certain that you will never drink again. If you hope you are going on holiday it doesn't mean you are going anywhere but if you know for certain, then you will definitely go. Once you make a firm decision, you cut off any other possibility and doubt; so whatever happens in your future life, drinking alcohol is not just not an option but something that you have no interest in doing. You have moved on and are free.

Let's make something very clear: the decision never to drink again is, without doubt, one of the most important decisions you will ever make. The reality is that both the length and the daily quality of your future life will depend on this decision. Some people say to me, 'Oh yeah, but you can get run over by a bus next week.' Of course you can, but would you take heroin because you could get run over by a bus next week and would you deliberately keep jumping in front of buses? Of course you wouldn't. There is a bus coming along for all of us but, in the meantime, it's the daily quality of our lives that counts, making sure we have our true courage, confidence and freedom every day.

Alcohol created so much fear in my mind that I simply thought there would be no point in living if I could not drink. Once I realised that I was, in a sense, my own jailer, the fears that had seemed so real and so strong proved to be false. Once it began to dawn on me that those unreal fears and insecurities were caused by alcohol, the decision never to drink again became the easiest I have ever made. I knew I was free even before I had my final drink and once I finished my last ever alcoholic drink, I jumped for joy. I had been questioning my drinking habit for weeks beforehand, asking myself if it was the drink that made the evening or the company. I watched other drinkers trying to justify why they needed that particular drink, even though it was only Monday night. I knew that it didn't do anything for me and I could see this clearly even before I stopped. On the morning after my final drink I felt terrible but, as I slowly awoke, the first thing I thought was 'I'm free!' It was one of the best feelings I have ever had and I have never lost it. I thought that it would be difficult for a few weeks but, far from it; I had made the concrete decision never to be dependent on alcohol again. Once you make that commitment, you're free.

I cannot stress enough just how easy it is to stop drinking and, when simplified, it really only comes down to a few things:

1. Decide never to drink alcohol again.

2. Don't sit around moping about it – celebrate your freedom.

3. Get some live nutrients flowing through your system in the first week.

That's it. It really can be that simple. It is only the indecision and regret that makes it difficult. The withdrawal from alcohol is no more than a hangover lasting a little longer than a day and we have all dealt with many of those in the past, although perhaps become immune to recently. If you start with a feeling of excitement and freedom you won't even be aware of it. You will be too relieved and happy to be bothered about any brief physical withdrawal. It is the doubt and uncertainty that causes the pangs which some people describe as withdrawal but it is all in the mind. This is why it is so important to start in a happy frame of mind so that the period of adjustment will be easy and enjoyable. I have said that it is important to read this entire book as that way you will find freedom not only easy and enjoyable to achieve but, most importantly, it will be permanent. If you have understood the trap at this stage I cannot blame you for being like Mr Itch of Itching Town to break free, but please wait. It is essential that you fully understand ...

The Adjustment Period

Some people call this the withdrawal period but with-drawal from what? Your body has never craved alcohol and never will. It has only ever wanted to get rid of the poison. The word 'withdrawal' itself can give the impression of trauma and a degree of pain. That is what a hangover is, the body doing its best to get rid of the poison for you. It is simply a way of keeping you alive. In truth the physical withdrawal is a good thing too as it is the body's way of healing itself. First it throws out the poison in the gut and liver, then, as time goes on, it releases all the toxins collected from alcohol that it has stored out of harm's way in its cells. It is purging the poison from your body and with it goes any remaining brainwashing from your mind. If you are a heavy drinker and your body shakes slightly after you stop, this is just a part of the process of eliminating the poison which happens incredibly quickly. If you see it for what it is you may even enjoy the process as it is evidence of your body healing itself. We now know that any physical aggravation after the first morning is very subtle and will be gone within ten days but for most people it is only three days. The mental adjustment lasts slightly longer but, in reality, can be the most enjoyable part of stopping drinking.

Let me explain. If you have a car for a few years and the indicators are on one side of the steering column and windscreen wipers on the other, isn't it true that when you buy another car they always seem to be on the opposite side? It's sod's law. What happens when you want to indicate? The windscreen wipers come on. Did you want to turn them on? No, you wanted to indicate. So why didn't you? It is because your brain has been conditioned for so long that it does it automatically. It just needs a little while to adjust and this takes from one to three weeks. After that, things become even clearer. This happens when you are mentally and physically completely outside the trap.

Let me ask you a question. If you made the mistake of putting on your wipers instead of indicating, would you stare at the wipers and say to yourself, 'Oh no, I can't get the hang of this new car. I will never adjust. I must get my old car back'? Of course you wouldn't. Would you even worry about it? Would you give it a second thought? The reality is that you laugh when you put the wipers on instead of the indicators and do it every ten minutes the first day. Does it bother you? Of course not. It simply comes down to the fact that you are not just hoping that your brain and body will adjust, you know for certain that they will. The knowing for certain has destroyed any doubt and that is why it doesn't bother you in the slightest. That is how powerful a sense of certainty really is. That is why, after you finish your final drink, you will know it is over rather than hope that it might be over. Whether you find it easy or not depends on how you think.

You have been conditioned to take drink at certain times depending on just how far into the trap you are. It can range from first thing in the morning to weekends, lunchtime, with dinner, when you come in from work, at celebrations or any other time. The point I am making is that, after you stop, you will still be coming home from work, still socialising, still eating (of course) and still waking up. That is why you need to understand that your brain and body will easily adjust, providing you let them and providing you don't worry about it. Any triggers that may occur over the first few weeks work in exactly the same way as the wiper-indicator situation. These are times to feel relieved and excited.

Every now and then you may get 'I want a drink' thoughts. They are nothing to worry about and are only thoughts. We do not act on all our thoughts as, if we did, most of us would be in jail! It is just understanding these thoughts that makes the whole business of stopping easy, enjoyable and permanent. If you ever think you want a drink it doesn't mean that something is going wrong; it is just the mental windscreen wipers flicking back to the old pattern for a split second. If you say to yourself 'I mustn't have one,' 'I can't have one' or 'When will I be free?' you will be defeating the whole object of the exercise and become a whinging ex-drinker. Just indicate, adjust, rejoice and move on. This is one of the most enjoyable aspects of stopping. These are the times when you can remind yourself that you don't need to do that any more because you're free. You can and will enjoy these moments if or when triggers occur over the first couple of weeks. This is adjustment and not willpower. Do not confuse them.

Willpower involves constantly fighting a desire to do something that you still want to do. If you allow yourself to think for one second that you are using will-power, you will start to doubt and where there is doubt there is uncertainty and where there is uncertainty there is always an element of willpower. Now this is really important. If you experience the trigger 'I want a drink' and you believe that the alcohol itself will benefit you in any way, then you have missed the point. You will switch on to willpower and be back in the pit in no time at all. If you experience the trigger 'I want a drink' and you know that there are genuinely no benefits, you will understand that it is simply a trigger that will be dismissed as quickly as you would turn off your wipers and put on the indicator. Will I have to do this all of my life? Of course not. You will retune yourself easily many times during the first couple of weeks and will love the process so much that it will become automatic. Using willpower is only necessary when you have to resist what you want.

See this adjustment for what it is. You are starving a disease to death. You are now in charge of something that was controlling you. That is exactly how I saw it. I had been feeding a disease that was controlling many aspects of my life because I was fooled into thinking that it was my friend. I thought it was helping me to enjoy life more and to cope with stress. When I realised that it always did the complete opposite and that it created the feelings of insecurity, I rejoiced in starving it to death. I did not use willpower, because I did not want to feed it. I wanted it out of my life for good. If you see it like this you will love the adjustment period because what is there to feel miserable about? Nothing. The sad reality of any drug addiction is that it is the addict who has to use ongoing willpower, discipline and control and it can last for life. Once the nature of this drug is fully understood there is no need for willpower, discipline or control. You will finally be free from having to exercise control.

At the beginning of one of my consultations a man said, 'It would be so nice if you could just put me a couple of weeks into the future, so that the worst is over.' By the end of the session he wanted the adjustment period just so that he could witness the disease starving to death. He wanted to kill it as he wanted some revenge. He realised that the worst was already over and he didn't need or want drink any more. As he put it, 'What would be the point?' Another common misconception is that if you are truly free from alcohol then you should no longer even think about drinking. This can also create doubt if not fully understood. So let me now cover the very important point which is that you will definitely ...

Think Drink

You will be thinking about drinking quite a lot over the first few weeks but it is what you think that makes the difference. I remember on one of my many attempts to abstain for a week, all I could think about was drink and the day I could start drinking again. I felt miserable and deprived and had a mental tantrum all week. Thinking about drinking was not the problem; it was how I was thinking. When I did finally stop completely I also thought about drinking but did so from a new perspective. I did not have a mental tantrum and was not staying in and complaining. Every time I thought about drinking I was elated to be free and couldn't wait to go out and prove, not only to myself but to the world, that I did not need alcohol.

A very common mistake that people make when attempting to kick the drink is trying not to think of alcohol or worrying about it if they are. Have you ever tried to do that? Have you ever tried not to think of something? It is impossible. The fact that you are trying not to means that you are thinking about it. Let me try an experiment. Try not to think of Paul McCartney. What are you thinking about right now? The point I'm making is that you will think about alcohol after you stop but it really is only what you think that makes the difference. Do you believe that Nelson Mandela never thought about the prison he was in for twenty-seven years after he was released? Of course he did. In fact he probably thought about it a lot more during the first few weeks after his release but does it mean that if he thought about it he must have secretly missed it? Of course not. Do you believe he ever thought, 'Oh I'd love to go back there, just for my birthday; what a shame I can't'? You must be joking! Especially if he knew that, if he did, it would be to spend the rest of his life there. Every time he thought about prison it must have been 'Isn't it wonderful, I'm free' and sheer relief to know that he was no longer being controlled but in control.

That is exactly how I think about alcohol now and I think about alcohol a lot, as you can imagine. It's the nature of what I do and it is my mission to cure the world of this disease but I never think I'm missing out, therefore I never have a problem. I am just so grateful that I saw it when I did and that I am now in control every day. To think that I am missing out now, I would have to lie to myself and convince myself that I was being deprived. That would be impossible because I understand the con and, once you know how any trick works, you will never be able to believe the illusion again. Nobody could ever convince me otherwise as, once you know the truth, you cannot be fooled.

As I explained in the chapter on advertising, it would be almost impossible to forget alcohol. It is the most advertised and accepted drug in the world and at the moment around 80 per cent of people in the UK alone are hooked. It is the attitude towards drinking that is the key to success in giving it up. Seeing it for what it actually is acts as a wonderful reminder of just how relieved you will feel to be free.

If you think about alcohol over the first few weeks, does it matter? You were thinking about alcohol a lot more than you realised anyway. I will repeat this a thousand times. Alcohol addicts, whether consciously or not, have to exercise willpower, discipline and some degree of control most of the time. It is only certain restrictions that prevent them from increasing their intake and making their descent to the bottom slightly slower. The rate of descent will vary from one drinker to the next because of the restrictions they impose and their body's ability to cope with the poisonous drug. However, they are all going in one direction ... down.

I think about heroin sometimes as it is frequently mentioned in the news. I simply think what a shame it is for those poor addicts. That is exactly how I think about alcohol now. I feel even sadder when I realise that most people are unaware of the fact that they are sinking and when I think about alcohol now it's 'How come I didn't see it earlier as it is all so obvious?' Alcohol is a drug like any other and, once you see it for what it is and are relieved to be free, it would not matter if you thought about alcohol twenty-four hours a day as you would still be happy.

Another big mistake people make when they stop drinking is that they try to avoid ...

Tempting Situations

What tempting situations are we talking about? There aren't any, they don't exist. If you were pulled from quicksand would you need to avoid certain situations in case you were tempted to jump back in? If you don't want or need to drink and are relieved to be free, why would you need to avoid these situations? The beauty of understanding the nature of the alcohol trap is that you do not have to avoid any situations. One of the key methods in this book is to make certain you don't. Every single moment that we have is to be savoured and not avoided.

When I was on the wagon for those three months I tried to avoid certain situations where I thought I would be tempted to drink. I avoided going out and socialising and when I did, I felt even more miserable than before. I still thought that I was missing out. I felt a lot more tempted to drink at those times than at any other but if you are tempted, you are tempted. If you believe you are making a genuine sacrifice then the advice to avoid situations where you might be tempted is ridiculous anyway. For how long exactly should you avoid social occasions? Well according to organisations like AA, it's forever. That's a pretty daunting prospect isn't it? It really would confirm your belief that life is dull, boring and miserable without alcohol. This will in turn create even greater feelings of deprivation causing you to feel more than tempted to have a drink, and this is what they call recovery. I call it penury. That is exactly what happened to me during those three months. The advice is even more stupid when you realise that some people are tempted to drink when they first wake up so does this mean they should never wake up again to avoid temptation? I suppose that would certainly solve their drink problem once and for all.

I cannot stress this point enough. There is no need whatsoever to avoid any situation that comes along. In fact it is important that you don't, as it sends your brain completely the wrong message and you will start to think that life is not as enjoyable without a drink. People often ask 'Should I avoid pubs?' Why? That would be the same as vegetarians avoiding restaurants in case they are tempted to have a T-bone steak. Vegetarians are not tempted to eat meat even if everybody else is, regardless of where they are. They cannot be tempted because they do not want meat. There is no need at all to avoid any situation, including pubs, as the real pleasure you get is from the companionship. You may, however, find yourself no longer wanting to visit pubs all the time because when you are sober, you start to notice things like flock wallpaper and floral carpets, cigarette burns, the stench of alcohol, the mood changes and the overall dingy atmosphere of many of them. In fact, I think that many pubs should be renamed to give them a more realistic feel. For example, instead of 'Ye Old Inn,' 'The White Horse' and 'The Crown and Anchor,' how about 'Ye Old Vomit Inn' or 'The Clown and Wanker' and 'The Violent Tavern'?

Am I suggesting that all pubs are like this? No, I'm not but you do need to realise that the main point of pubs is to enable people to get their drug fix. I still go to pubs, wine bars and clubs. If I am having a great time, excellent; if not, I know that a drink will not make the evening better as I realise that it is just a lousy evening or I am not in the mood. I am never genuinely tempted to drink. In fact it's just the opposite. I go for the company, to socialise and have fun though this can sometimes be difficult in your regular run-down, dingy local. Once you are sober and physically and mentally free, you will start to see just how much more to life there really is.

Remember you stop drinking, not living. Once the poison has left your mind and body completely, it will not matter if it's New Year, your birthday or a holiday as you simply will not miss drink. You will be able to celebrate just like you used to with dancing, good company, fireworks, good friends, laughter, having a blast. The difference will be that you will remember the entire evening and will wake up feeling refreshed and alive. The added bonus will be that you will always be able to drive yourself home.

This is another huge part of the alcohol problem, not only in this country but around the world. The brainwashing is so severe that the word 'celebrate' is linked to a drug; that drug being alcohol. This is because, from the moment we are born, we have been subjected to thousands of images of people celebrating all kinds of events with alcohol. Whether it's a birthday or a lottery win, drinkers will look for any excuse to celebrate, which means having a drink. Sport is always a good one. If your team wins, have a drink. If your team loses, have a drink. One is to celebrate, the other to drown your sorrows. If you do win the lottery, the first thing the organisers do is bring you a bottle of champagne (which is nothing more than a hyped up, fizzy, gone off fruit anyway). We have been so conditioned to link alcohol with celebration that the English footballer I spoke of earlier was even presented with a bottle of champagne for winning 'Man of the Match' after he had told the world that he was an alcoholic. Were they on a wind-up?

A woman once came to see me for a group session to stop smoking. At the end of it she was the only one in the small group who didn't look very excited, which is unusual. I asked her if she looked forward to being a non-smoker and her answer came as something of a shock. 'I was feeling really good, until you told me to go out and celebrate.' I said, 'What on earth is wrong with going out to celebrate and why wouldn't you want to?' She replied, 'I am a recovering alcoholic and you have just told me to have a drink. That is very inconsiderate of you and I now realise that I cannot truly celebrate.' I must admit, I thought I was hearing things. I had never once told her to go out and have a drink to celebrate; I had simply said 'celebrate.' I had almost forgotten that nearly everyone links that word with alcohol.

The singer Eric Clapton holds an annual New Year's Eve party where all the guests are ex-addicts of some kind. He feels he cannot celebrate with normal people and holds the party for people in a similar situation to himself. Why can't he celebrate with people who drink alcohol? What's stopping him? It is only one thing and that is his belief. While he believes he is abnormal for not drinking and that people who drink are normal, then he will always feel vulnerable. He will feel as though it's something in him and not the nature of the drug. Celebration equals alcohol for the vast majority of people in this country as the two just go together.

I used to believe this too but not any more. I am now in the same position as I was before I was sucked in by this confidence trick. I celebrate by having nice people around me with good music and laughter; just having a good time and feeling good about the day or situation. It is sad to think that the woman at my clinic believes that she is still recovering from alcohol yet she hasn't had a drink in three years. It is even sadder to think that she believes the only thing she can ever celebrate is the fact that she has stayed sober for that day, but in her mind she cannot even celebrate that because, to her, celebration means having a drink. She is not alone as nearly everyone does this. Make sure you don't avoid any social situation as this is, without doubt, the best part of the method. It is one of my key instructions.

You will start to notice your windscreen wipers coming on every now and then (to refer to my earlier analogy) but you will also understand that, by building a mental muscle, you are reversing the massive alcohol brainwashing which has made you, me and millions like us victims of a very clever confidence trick. Remember, the pain of stopping drinking is a myth; it is all in the mind. It is easy to stop drinking. It was only the feeling of deprivation that created the myth of 'recovery.' It was the feeling of 'missing out' that caused you to avoid situations when trying to stop or cut down in the past. Not only do you no longer need to avoid situations but, for the first time, you can enjoy more of them, more frequently, with an added sense of freedom and joy in the knowledge that you are no longer a slave to a drug but truly free to live your life as you now choose.

So, enjoy going out for a 'non-drink' and enjoy not needing a drink. It is a wonderful feeling and one that never goes away. Enjoy being in control and rejoice in your freedom. You will not be free if you are avoiding situations, so don't avoid them; be totally free to participate knowing that you are in charge.

Another question that people often ask me is, 'What do I drink instead of alcohol?' The question seems logical enough but another very important part of this method is to realise that you do not need and should not search for any kind of ...

Replacements

One of the key instructions essential to success is that you

**DO NOT SEARCH FOR A
REPLACEMENT FOR ALCOHOL.**

We must get it clear in our minds that we do not need to drink anything alcoholic when we are socialising. Some people say, 'There are only so many orange juices you can drink.' It's funny that they don't say the same thing with alcoholic drinks, isn't it?

The addiction is a disease and the disease ends the second you stop taking the drug alcohol. If you had a different progressive disease that was only going to get worse and you found a cure, would you be searching for a replacement for that disease after you were cured or would you simply breathe a sigh of relief not to have the disease any more? I know what I would do, which is exactly what I do quite often. I breathe a sigh of relief not to have to suffer mentally or physically any longer.

Why would anyone want a replacement for a disease? It doesn't make sense. People only want a replacement if they think they are missing out on a genuine pleasure. It's only because they still feel deprived. When people are driving, for example, they are forced not to drink alcohol, so they drink non-alcoholic beers and wines.

The only reason for this is because they feel as though they have made a sacrifice. During the three months that I gave up, I tried loads of non-alcoholic beers and wines but couldn't get to like them. This was simply because they contained no alcohol.

If you were to switch to non-alcoholic beer or wine, especially during the adjustment period, there is a danger that, subconsciously, you would be impressing on your mind that you had made a genuine sacrifice. This could act like a dripping tap and make you believe you were missing out on something. If you were to drink these non-alcoholic drinks it would be exactly the same as an addict quitting heroin but continuing to inject themselves with a substance that cost the same amount as heroin, looked like heroin, felt like heroin, but had no heroin in it. Do you think that this would help them free themselves or drive them insane? Obviously, it would drive the addict insane because the only reason for seeking a replacement in the first place was the feeling of missing out.

As for the statement 'There are only so many orange juices you can drink,' there are millions of delicious drinks that do not contain alcohol. I drink plenty of them when I'm out and at home. We need to drink as it is part of our survival mechanism but we should only drink if we are thirsty. The reason that I could drink so much alcohol was because it was dehydrating me, so much so that I felt thirsty all the time. When you stop dehydrating your body, you will realise that you just don't need to drink all the time as a couple of drinks can last you all night.

I'm not saying that there aren't going to be times when water just isn't going to cut it, but there are many, many non-alcoholic drinks on the market like Amé, Purdey's or Appletiser that really do taste pretty good. Also I'm not saying that everyone will hate the taste of non-alcoholic wines and beers, I'm just saying that most of them are full of rubbish and there is a danger that you could easily send subconscious messages to your brain suggesting you're missing out, which is the last thing you would want.

There are many 'experts' who will tell you that if you stop drinking you need to replace it with something else. Like what? Meetings every week, perhaps? You will find that, after a while, you will have new interests, not as a result of replacing alcohol but because you are expanding your life and broadening your horizons. When you don't need to drink you will want to do a lot more with your life. This is not replacement, it's living. If you think you would prefer these non-alcoholic beers and wines because drinking orange juice doesn't look very adult, then grow up. It was precisely that kind of thinking that got us trapped in the first place. People think that it doesn't look cool to drink a soft drink but it isn't very cool to get stupid, aggressive, argumentative, obnoxious, violent, uptight, hostile, fall over, slur your words, collapse, blow your mind or throw up either. You see, it's all in the mind fed on adverts. Anyway, who's to know that the tonic and lemon doesn't have a vodka in it?

'A pint of orange juice is the same price as a pint of beer, so what's the point in switching to soft drinks as it will cost just as much.' What's the point? The point is to be free from drug addiction and it won't cost anywhere near the same amount as being an alcohol addict. As I have already said, alcohol dehydrates the body making you drink more and besides, money is not a factor for alcohol drinkers who buy it for the effect of the drug. Having all the money in the world means nothing if you are a slave to a substance.

It is now very clear to me and will soon become just as clear to you, if it hasn't already, that you were substituting when you were drinking. You were replacing real courage, real confidence, real relaxation and the real you with a false substitute. One of the joys of stopping is to not have to substitute or replace any more.

So now you realise that there is no genuine pleasure to be had in alcohol. You realise that it causes insecurities and stress, destroys your courage, undermines your confidence and is incapable of providing any genuine relaxation. You also realise that you are suffering from a progressive disease that will only get worse and worse. You are in the trap and, whether you knew it or not before you picked up this book, it is now time to gain the ultimate freedom from this slavery. You will have complete freedom from a disease that was undermining every area of your life, whether you were conscious of it or not. It is a confidence trick on a massive scale, in fact, the biggest one ever to plague mankind. Now that you can see it for what it is, it is time to get very excited and time to realise that you do not have to continue drinking. It is now time to decide when you are going to have ...

The Final Drink

It all sounds very final doesn't it? The 'final drink' suggests sacrifice, or it would do to 80 per cent of our population, but it won't to you. Any fear that you may have at this moment is also mixed with adrenalin and excitement. As I have already explained, there is nothing to fear at all, as it was all false in the first place. Fear is the biggest part of the con trick as the very nature of alcohol makes people feel insecure without it and that's exactly what keeps them hooked.

There is nothing final about that final drink; it simply spells a new beginning. You are achieving not only what you want to achieve but, in reality, what most drinkers would love and that is to be able to enjoy and cope with life without having to drink; to be physically and mentally free from drug addiction forever. Just imagine how it would feel to no longer be dependent.

We have been conditioned into thinking that being truly free from alcohol is impossible to achieve. We have been taught to believe in this mythical disease known as 'alcoholism' for which there is no known cure. We have been taught that, if you do stop drinking, you will only be able to expect a satisfactory way of life. This is simply because, to alcohol addicts, stopping drinking is like losing a close friend. This would be true if you thought that alcohol was always there when you needed it and always helped you cope with the stresses and strains of life. All this recovery nonsense is nothing more than a broken heart and people say there is no cure for that, but of course there is.

When a close friend or relative dies we have to go through a mourning process. There is no physical pain but it is a real trauma and can take years to get over. Even then, there is a void that can last for the rest of our lives. This is what drinkers put themselves through when they stop. This is why they believe there is no cure and why they fear the prospect of that final drink. They feel they are parting with an old friend and, as far as they are concerned, it really does spell the end. They will experience a void for years after they have stopped and in some ways it is even worse for the poor drinker than for the person who really has lost a close friend. At least when a close friend dies, you can start the mourning process and, after time, your brain will accept that they are gone. The poor drinker thinks their old companion is still out there but they cannot be friends any more because they abused it. What's worse is that everybody else can enjoy the benefits of this friend but they can't. That is because we are taught that if you abuse alcohol you will pay the price.

Abuse alcohol? It was alcohol that inflicted the abuse. It was never the other way around. Alcohol addicts who give up will start with a feeling of doom and gloom and that feeling may stay with them forever. However, they are not losing a friend but getting rid of a disease that would have affected their quality of life forever. By stopping drinking you are breaking free and achieving something that most drinkers would love. Have fun, rejoice in your freedom and enjoy letting that disease starve to death.

I once read a book called *The Effective Way to Stop Drinking* written by Beauchamp Colclough. It is a catalogue of doom and gloom. I am not directly criticising Colclough; in fact I feel sorry for him as he honestly believes he is a recovering alcoholic and, because he believes it, he is. In his book he states: 'Alcoholism is a fatal disease if it's not arrested. I use the word "arrested" because there is no cure. A lot of people seem to think that, if you don't drink alcohol for a period of time, they will be able to continue drinking again. That is not the case. When a person with a drinking problem puts down the drink, the consequences surrounding the drinking problem cease; if that person picks up a drink again. Then he or she has got the problem back. It doesn't go away.'

What does he mean it doesn't go away? Of course the disease goes away. The chemical addiction to any drug is a disease that gets worse and worse. If you stop putting the cause of the disease into your body then you are cured. It is essential to understand that you have a disease in order to cure it but isn't it just as important to know when you are cured? In reality, Beauchamp is not fully cured. He has no alcohol in his body but still believes that he is making a sacrifice as he is still fighting a desire to do something he doesn't ever want to do again.

To the Colcloughs, Skinners or Bests of this world, the final drink spells the death of a friend and the beginning of a battle that has to be fought every day for the rest of their lives. Is it any wonder they feel so afraid to stop? Is it any surprise they feel so low when they do stop? When I stopped six years ago I knew it was going to be different before I had even consumed my last drink. I could see that moment for what it was; the ending of a disease and the beginning of my freedom. I looked forward to having my last drink, not for the drink but for knowledge that I was a 100 per cent certain it was my last. What a wonderful feeling it was; a feeling that has never gone away.

So when should you have your final drink? What is the best time? Should you have it alone, with friends, indoors, outdoors? The choice is now yours. You have your final drink wherever you choose to have it but make sure you have it. If you have already had your final drink and, as far as you are concerned, it's already over, then congratulations, you are now free. However, please finish this book as everything in it is here for a reason. If you haven't yet had your final drink, choose a time that suits you but don't put it off. If you have understood what is in this book and can see it clearly, then you won't want to put it off for a moment longer. If you are slightly apprehensive, which is normal, it is only the last remnant of the false fear that is keeping you trapped. This will be dispelled in no time at all as I explained in the period of adjustment chapter.

Whatever your views on alcohol were before you read this book, now is the time to dump them for good. Remember:

THE PAST DOES NOT EQUAL THE FUTURE.

It is what you do today that counts. So many people carry unwanted failures with them through life. They weigh them down with fear that they won't succeed today because of what happened yesterday. It's rubbish. You will succeed and it's easy. I have made a list of all the instructions. Follow them and freedom will be yours for the taking. It doesn't matter how long you have been drinking, what your intake is or how many times you have tried to stop. Anyone can find it easy and enjoyable to stop drinking. All you have to do is:

UNDERSTAND THE TRAP AND FOLLOW THE STEPS TO FREEDOM.

You must get it clear that knowledge is nothing without the final ingredient for your ultimate success which is action. So many people know what to do and how they can do it but fail to carry it out. It's not what you know but what you do with your knowledge that counts. It is no good knowing what to do without acting on it. Why wouldn't you want to? There is no downside to this decision, only an upside. What are the alternatives? Did you believe when you had your very first drink all those years ago that you would have to spend an indefinite number of years drinking? Did you ever think you would become dependent? When you had your first drink did you even consider that one day just the thought of stopping would put fear into you? Has it got better or worse? Unless you do stop this disease, what is there to stop you spending the rest of your life drinking?

I have already given you the instructions you need but, to simplify them, here are ...

The *True* Steps to Freedom

1. Decision

   Make your decision that, after the final drink, you
   will never drink alcohol again. I have explained
   just how powerful a genuine decision really is. It
   cuts off all other possibilities; it gives certainty
   that literally destroys any doubts. You must realise
   that you can easily achieve it. There is nothing different about you because the only person that can
   make you drink is you.

2. Nothing to give up

   Keep it clear in your mind that there is nothing to
   give up. I can understand that stopping drinking
   seems difficult if you think you are giving up a
   genuine pleasure or crutch but, once you realise
   there is nothing to give up, it's easy. I don't mean
   that the disadvantages outweigh the advantages;
   I mean that there are no advantages. All the
   apparent advantages, were just that – apparent.
   The courage, confidence, relaxation, pleasure, etc.
   were simply illusions based on the removal of
   our natural fears. The advantages never actually
   existed. That is why you would feel just as stupid
   moping around wanting an alcoholic drink after
   you stopped as you would searching for Santa
   Claus or fairies, because they do not exist. I have
   illustrated over and over again that alcohol will

exist for a long time but that all the things we were conditioned to believe alcohol did for us, do not exist. That was all you were hooked on – the illusions. So remember, there is nothing to give up and you are not making any sacrifice. It is the people who drink who make all the sacrifices.

3. Never say 'I can't'

    Constant And Never-ending Torture is precisely what 'recovery' is. Do you want to be in recovery, just surviving from day to day, or do you want to be fully liberated and living every day? Never say 'I can't have a drink' when you know full well that you can physically pick one up if you wanted to as there is nothing stopping you. You can inject yourself with heroin too, you just do not want to. You do not want to be a slave to alcohol any more, so don't torture yourself by saying 'can't.' Remove the T from the word and you have immediately removed the self-imposed torture, replacing it with Constant And Never-ending happiness.

4. Think drink

    Do not try not to think about alcohol or worry if you are thinking about it a lot of the time. It is impossible to try not to think of something. Just make sure, whenever you think about it, whether it is today, tomorrow, next week or for the rest of your life, that you think 'I don't have to do that any more, isn't it great, I'm free, I'm a non-drinker!' That way you can think about drinking every minute of the day and you will still be happy. It is what you think that makes the difference.

5.   There is no such thing as an alcoholic (as society understands it)

You must get it clear in your mind that there is no such thing as an alcoholic. Whether you thought you were one or not, your common sense should help you realise that there is no such thing. You are just a normal person who fell for a very clever confidence trick, just like millions of others all over the world but, unlike many others still stuck in this psychological trap, you are breaking free. Having made that decision to break free, never begin to torture yourself by doubting it. The disease only exists for the people who need to drink, not for those who don't.

6.   Do not feel down – Rejoice in your feedom

There is nothing to feel down about. Start off with a happy frame of mind. The second you finish your final drink, it's over. Rejoice from the start, because you are free from the start. Do not turn into a whinging ex-drinker, there is nothing worse. There is nothing to pine for and everything to feel happy about.

7.   Do not count days

What is the point? What are you going to do, count the days since you stopped for the rest of your life? How pathetic would that be? Almost as sad as the poor souls in AA who celebrate every year with a cake. The more candles you have on your cake the longer you have survived. You don't want to survive or hang on in there for the rest of your life, you want to live. So just do it – live. Leave alcohol behind, it's something that you used to do. Now you don't have to.

8. Do not avoid any situations

   You have stopped drinking, not living. Enjoy social gatherings from the start; they are so much more enjoyable when you are the real you.

9. Never say 'Just the one'

   Drinking alcohol is drug addiction and causes a chain reaction. See the whole business of drink for what it is, drug addiction and peddling on a massive scale. If you think there is genuine pleasure in one drink, you will think there is a genuine pleasure in a million. Face the fact that, whether you like it or not, you have a disease. It will not go away simply because you put your head in the sand. Like all crippling diseases, it not only lasts for life but gets worse and worse. The easiest time to cure it is now.

10. Do not use any replacements

   Avoid non-alcoholic beers or wines. These simply perpetuate the illusion that you have made a sacrifice.

11. Do not envy drinkers – Feel sorry for them

   Do not envy people who need to drink alcohol as there is absolutely nothing to envy. See drinkers as objects of pity, not envy. Most of them are not even aware that they are trapped. They have a progressive disease and feel dependent on a drug and most do not even know it. Is that something to envy? Once they realise that you are free and happy about stopping, they will probably envy you.

12. This is not a safety net

   Never think for one second that this method is a safety net. I will explain this in more detail in the final chapter – Final Warning.

Finally: Do follow all these steps. They are your guaranteed 'twelve steps' to freedom.

If you have understood all I have said and realised how simple the alcohol trap is and if you actually follow all the instructions then, in no time at all, you will receive the ...

Biggest Buzz in the World

The biggest buzz you will get from alcohol is when you no longer have to take it. The feeling is one of elation; a true mental and physical boost that is yours to recapture whenever you wish. This feeling will happen for you, if it hasn't happened already at some point during the adjustment period. I had the sense of joy and freedom even before I finished my final drink but the biggest buzz was yet to come. During the first few weeks after I had stopped, everything became so clear. It was at this stage that I realised alcohol did absolutely nothing for me. I was going out, having fun and most of the time I wasn't even thinking about drinking. When I did think about it I became happier and happier each day as I knew I never had to drink again. I could see this fairly clearly before I'd actually had my last drink but during the first couple of weeks I frequently experienced (and still do today) the biggest buzz in the world from not having to drink.

I must admit that I did suffer some physical pain when I stopped drinking including bruised legs when I kicked myself for not seeing it earlier. That, for me, was the most frustrating part. But it's like that damn Rubik's Cube; it only appears difficult if you go about it the wrong way. Once you have the solution everything falls into place. The reason for my frustration was that it was as though I had been locked in a prison for years then suddenly realised that I'd always had the key.

In the end I realised that I was my own jailer. I kept myself trapped by believing that there were genuine benefits in drinking alcohol and that alcohol was somehow different from any other drug. Realise that you are your own jailer as there is only one person who can make it difficult for you to stop drinking and that is you. The key is in your mind and this book is about showing you how to turn back the clock to the time before you even started drinking.

The moment of euphoria or 'the big buzz' will happen at some point during the first few weeks, if it hasn't already. This has nothing whatsoever to do with alcohol leaving your body but simply the adjustment I talked about. Do not sit around waiting for anything to happen, just get on with your life and enjoy purging the disease from your mind and body.

To be honest, it is very hard to describe just how wonderful it is to be free without coming across as evangelical. I just want to show the world that what they have believed for so long about alcohol is wrong. It is just one big illusion. I want everyone who is hooked to realise that they are. I want the world to see that alcohol creates insecurities while giving the illusion of courage. I want the drinking world to know that they are being conned.

If you are concerned that social gatherings, meals, birthdays, parties, holidays and lunches will not be the same without alcohol, then you are correct, they are not the same:

THEY ARE INFINITELY BETTER.

I feel alive again, awake again, clear headed again. Do you remember what it was like to be a child at a party; that sense of excitement and fun? That is what I feel like when I go out now. I just want to be social, to dance and have fun. When I felt dependent on alcohol, the number one priority was to make sure I had a drink, everything else came second. I even rated a party by the quality and quantity of drink available. Now I don't say things like, 'I will talk to you in a minute, just let me get a drink.'

My only question now is not why was it easy for me to stop drinking but why did I ever think it needed to be difficult? With an open mind and a few instructions, it's easy. Does this mean that all social gatherings are going to be brilliant from now on and there will be no low points? No. This book is about dealing with common sense and reality. Were all social occasions fun while you were drinking? No. Did you ever have bad days when you were drinking? Yes, of course. I am not saying that you will never have a bad time from now on. What I am saying is that, because you will be physically and mentally a lot stronger than you have been in years, any highs are much higher and any lows that do come along are not going to seem as low as they once were.

So, let yourself get excited. You are reclaiming your freedom and becoming free. When I first stopped drinking I used to hide the fact that I had stopped, such is the stigma around non-drinkers. I used to tell people that

I was driving or that I didn't feel like it at the moment or that I was taking medication. Now I want to tell the world and so should you. There is no need to be embarrassed about the fact that you no longer want or have to drink. How have we reached a stage in our society where we have to justify not needing a drug anyway?

Remember that the poor drinkers always have to justify their intake to themselves and everyone else. You no longer have to justify anything, so don't.

Every time I go out, I get a buzz from not having to drink. I think 'What a relief I don't have to do that any more.' You will too and you won't be able to help yourself. Although one part of you will feel genuinely sorry for drinkers, another will feel a sense of achievement, a sense of pride and of being slightly different and rebellious, a sense of exhilaration and one of real and genuine freedom.

Some people have described it as one of the best feelings they have ever had. Oh, the joy you have to look forward to. Don't wait for it to happen, the minute you finish that final drink, you cut off the supply and you are:

FREE AT THAT MOMENT.

Why wait to celebrate? If the whole object is to say 'Isn't it wonderful, I don't need to drink any more', then why not say it from the start? John McCarthy didn't wait to celebrate and neither did Nelson Mandela, so why should you? When I passed my driving test, I didn't avoid telling anyone in case I couldn't drive next week. I knew that by next week I would be a better driver than I was when I first passed. That is why, if anybody asks why you aren't drinking, you should tell them the truth from the start. Tell them 'Because I don't want to any more' or, more importantly, 'Because I don't have to any more.' If you do this then you can help me with my vocation in life which is to help every drinker in the world see alcohol addiction for what it actually is, so that we can finally …

End This Madness

On this tiny island alone, in the next fifteen to twenty minutes (and every fifteen to twenty minutes after that), there will be two drink-driving convictions and two emergency medical admissions, one admission to a psychiatric hospital and one death due to alcohol. As I write this line in this updated version of the book in September 2010, the *Daily Mail* had the headline 'Drinking puts 1,500 in hospital every day.' The article reports on a new study from Liverpool John Moores University which states that in 2008/9, 606,799 people were admitted to hospital with drink related problems. Some were treated more than once, leading to 945,469 total admissions. It is worth noting that visits to casualty units were NOT included in this figure. This would have taken the toll to way over one million people! Between 2006 and 2008, liver disease alone claimed the lives of more than 11,000 men. Cirrhosis has increased tenfold since the first edition of this book was published and in 2009/10, alcohol was responsible for nearly half a million crimes in England. The report also says that alcohol is now responsible for around 15,000 deaths a year but there is no question that the real figure is even higher. Professor Mark Bellis, one of authors of this damning report, is quoted as saying: 'The price we pay for turning a blind eye to the real extent of alcohol abuse across England is reflected in the new Local Alcohol Profiles for England and it is a price that is paid especially by the poorest communities.' He also adds: 'It is time to recognise that we are not a population of responsible drinkers with just a handful of irresponsible individuals ruining it for others.' It is said that it's those who abuse alcohol who have the problems but nobody ever abuses alcohol; alcohol always abuses its victim as well as its collateral victims. Any form of drug addiction physically and mentally abuses its victim; it is never the other way round.

Alcohol probably kills well over a million people around the world every year. Nobody knows the exact figure as it is so hard to gauge. Every day it destroys millions of lives in so many different ways. In 2009 our own government earned over £8.7 billion from a disease we know kills 9,000 of its own people every year and destroys the quality of life of millions of others. The industry is allowed to spend over £200 million every year advertising this drug in the UK. Alcohol is responsible for more suicides, more murders, more rapes, more beatings, more physical and verbal violence, more sexual abuse, more divorces, more financial ruin and a general reduction of quality and length of life both for the addict and those around them than any other drug in the world. What is more, it is legal. Even our children's lives are being shaped by passive drinking as we speak.

Alcohol drags society down in ways that have never truly been understood until now. It is the biggest confidence trick to fool mankind ever and it must be stopped.

You will now do your bit to help just by being free. You are literally at the start of a massive shift in society's perception of alcohol. You are one of the elite, one of the few who can now see alcohol for what it really is. You are the new advertising campaign. We are only just beginning to change our perception and attitude towards the world's most used and accepted drug. You can help me to help others become aware of the trap they are in, so they too can be free and it is not just accepted that future generations will become dependent on the drug. It should not be the 'norm' to drink alcohol but the other way round.

Just by gaining your freedom, you will be helping to shift attitudes to alcohol in the same way as happened with smoking. Smoking was also seen as 'cool,' 'big,' sociable and an adult thing to do for many years. The perception of smoking is now very different. At one time over 60 per cent of the population was smoking; it is now 30 per cent and dropping. Alcohol needs to go the same way because passive drinking destroys more lives than passive smoking ever did. Alcohol does nothing but destroy people mentally and physically. I am just a normal person who has found freedom but I believe I am the most passionate person in the world about this subject, and I will do everything in my power to help as many people as I can to break free from this slavery. My vocation is to cure the world of this disease.

What is the best way you can contribute? It is simply by being you – going out as usual, enjoying meals as usual and doing all the things you always did. When others see that it is possible to be free, when they see that you can easily enjoy life to the full without alcohol and they see that you don't need it, when they see you looking better and feeling better, they will realise. When they see that you have more confidence and, more courage, that you are more relaxed and that your life has improved in every single area, they will want to be part of it too. It's contagious.

Do not become a 'holier than thou' ex-drinker as there really is nothing worse. Always remember that you were there once so do not be too quick to judge. Anybody who is getting drunk around you is not choosing to drink; they have to drink. Just because they believe it's their choice does not change the reality. This is why prohibition did not work and never could work. You cannot solve the alcohol problem by banning it or trying to pretend it is not there. Once you have been deluded by alcohol, insecurities inevitably follow. The addict is then duped into thinking that they cannot enjoy or cope with life without alcohol. Choice does not come into it which is why it is no good giving drinkers an ultimatum like 'Either the drink goes or I go.' The poor addict will pick the drink, not because they choose to but because they have to. They feel as though coping without you would be less painful than coping without their crutch. If you ban alcohol, drinkers will want it even more as it becomes the CAN'T syndrome on a massive scale or the forbidden 'gone off' fruit.

All you need to know is that most drinkers you meet, whatever the situation, will secretly envy you. They will want it even more when they see just how happy you are to be free. Some will expect you to get uptight about not drinking and expect you to mope around or at least whinge a bit. However, they will realise that you are not opting out of life but going out and enjoying yourself just as before. They will think that you are incredible, unique, special and superhuman. The most important part is that you will be feeling these things yourself.

The drinkers around you will want to be part of it. I am seeing a change around me all the time. People who before wouldn't even have contemplated giving up drinking are now either stopping or at least questioning their drinking like never before. They may not say publicly that they want to be free for fear they couldn't achieve it but the effect you will have on those same people will be contagious. Everyone will soon want to know how you did it. You can start your own revolution.

It may take time for society to make this shift in attitude but it will happen. When it does you will know that you have helped in that process. You will help others realise that people just do not need alcohol. Then, instead of them dragging you down, you will lift them up. However, you cannot force anyone to stop. There are still members of my family who drink (they haven't read this book yet!). This is painful for me as I can see they are in a sinking ship and missing out on the juice of life. Yet, if I were to throw them a life jacket I know they would simply toss it back to me. It is not that they are being difficult; it's because of the fear and insecurity created by the drug that keeps them hooked. It takes a lot for people to read this book or come to my clinic for a session. I admire you for overcoming your fears, reading the whole book and making the concrete decision to break free for the rest of your life.

You now realise that there is no reason why anyone should find it difficult to stop drinking. It is so easy when all the brainwashing and illusions have been removed but please remember that others may not understand – yet. So, if you were to turn into an evangelist, you would not be helping them, nor does it help to pressure them. Simply be yourself and enjoy your freedom. They will soon pick up the book and, like you, be in a position where they can finally take control of their own lives and experience a full and enjoyable ...

LIFE

LIVE IN FEARLESS EXCITEMENT.

One of the biggest joys of being free is the sudden realisation that everything we will ever need is within us already. We have the ability to meet every challenge. We have the courage to overcome any fears. We have the capability to feel joy and happiness at a moment's notice. We have the finest drug in the world in its purest form already within us and it's free of charge. It is called the life force. It is the buzz we get from being alive, growing every day and embracing new opportunities. Alcohol literally destroys that life force. It slowly makes you die inside. If you are not growing, you are dying; there is no in-between. Drinkers have no idea just how much the drug is affecting them or how much it rules so many aspects of their lives. They look around and see that they are pretty much the same as everyone else. That is the problem; you don't want to be the same as the majority of the population, you want to be ALIVE, not just 'another brick in the wall' as the Pink Floyd song goes. Most people are missing out on the juice of life. Most people survive but don't really live. Most people have stress but not challenges. Most people are hooked.

Stress only becomes stress if you are not strong enough to handle it. A drinker will always be more mentally and physically stressed than they would be if they didn't drink. Wouldn't it be lovely if there were a product which could:

- Help us relieve stress in an instant

- Give us courage in an instant

- Generate confidence in an instant

- Make us happy and joyous in an instant

- Relax us in an instant

- Improve our social skills in an instant

Drinkers are deluded into believing that alcohol can do all this and more. Not only does alcohol not provide any of the above but it does the exact opposite.

The good news is that there is something that can achieve all these things in an instant and it is called the mind. How we think creates every emotion we have and all of us have the ability instantly to tap into any emotion. Children do not need alcohol if they get stressed yet one of the most stressful periods for any human being is early childhood. Unfortunately many children are affected by passive drinking, so the natural tendency is for them to reach for their own kind of escapism at some point. The illusions created by the drug confirm their conditioning that alcohol will provide them with their needs and their genuine courage and confidence are destroyed early on. It happens so slowly for most that they don't even realise it. The sad thing is that they believe the opposite; that alcohol is giving them courage and confidence when, in fact, they are slowly dying inside.

Without challenge or fear in your life you have no grounds on which to build or use courage. Without courage you can never grow, you can never learn and build. Without fear you slowly wither away inside. Alcohol destroys courage. It removes natural fears and creates additional fears and insecurities that shouldn't be there. It slowly kills people physically but, more importantly, it kills them emotionally, little by little each day. Challenges or stress are wonderful tools to help shape you and make you who you are. You will now start to grow in ways beyond your comprehension and be much better equipped to take them on as stress is an emotion like any other without which you wouldn't grow. Challenge is now like a game I cannot lose because the person I am can never be taken away. We are born with the gift of emotion and happiness, love, joy and fulfilment are ours in a second if we want them. When you drink alcohol you rely on it to provide you with these emotions but it never does. Alcohol does the complete opposite.

I have seen people who stop drinking but go on to replace it with another drug. You do not need a replacement for drug addiction and you definitely do need a replacement for a disease that simply gets worse and worse and eventually becomes a living nightmare. If you feel you need another drug to replace alcohol then you have missed the whole point. You definitely do not need any drug. Everything we need for fulfilment, joy and happiness is right here, within us. We can have them whenever we wish, if we just tap into our inner resources.

> You definitely do not need any drug.
> Everything we need for fulfilment, joy and happiness is right here, within us.

Life could be a hundred year long holiday. Sometimes people believe they got a lousy deal; that their tour operator went bust, leaving them with a holiday from hell. What they fail to realise is that we are our own tour operators which means we can design the holiday of our dreams, so take charge of your life each and every day. We are all so busy working for tomorrow that we sometimes fail to appreciate today, this moment and each second of our lives. Many people play the 'I'll be happy when … ' game: 'I'll be happy when I earn this amount of money,' 'I'll be happy when I get this new car', 'I'll be happy when I reach the top,' etc. Always living in the future misses the present. I still play the 'I'll be happy when … .' game, but I've changed the rules slightly. Now I'll be happy when … ever I want.

Life means life and now that you are breaking free you will always feel more alive both mentally and physically. This gives you the resources to tap into a quality of life you had forgotten even existed. Alcohol drags people down so much that they simply accept an inferior way of life. I had no idea just how much alcohol was affecting every area of my life because it happened so gradually and I was comparing myself to other people. I can now compare myself to my old self. I now have more money, much better health, more peace of mind, more self-respect, more courage, more confidence and so much more physical and mental energy that it's a joke. As well as that, I have my true freedom back again. I'm me and loving it.

Enjoy your freedom and never go back to drug addiction, no matter how long you have stopped. The facts about alcohol never change. Enjoy the highs and learn from the lows.

To make sure that you have lifelong success here is ...

The Final Warning

The book is rarely ever the same twice. I just want to repeat that again as it is a very important part of the book …

The book is rarely ever the same twice.

It is easy to stop drinking and to stay stopped, providing you understand that the book is rarely the same twice. I cannot repeat this point enough. I have said that if you follow all the steps then you will be free forever. You need to understand this point more than any other. It's easy to stop drinking but it is mental and physical torture to try to control it. This is because alcohol is a drug and the nature of any drug is to take more and more. If you ever believe that you want to control it, you have missed the point. It means that you haven't fully understood the nature of the beast 'alcohol.' Remember that you no longer want to have to exercise control which is precisely why you stopped.

The only danger with this book is that it could make it easy to stop. How can that be a danger? People who find it easy to stop can find it easy to start again. This is a category you do not want to find yourself in as the book will not work a second time. This is because the book is rarely the same twice.

If you were ever curious enough to have a drink and thought to yourself, 'Just one won't hurt. After all it was so easy to stop that even if I did get hooked again, it wouldn't matter as I now have a way out. I will simply re-read the book.' NO NO NO NO NO NO NO NO NO NO NO NO NO NO NO NO NO NO NO NO NO NO!

The information in this book is new to you at this moment. What I mean is that it has been presented in such a way that your brain responds by thinking, 'Wow, I have never seen it that way before. That makes so much sense.' This book is designed to inspire and excite you because of its sheer simplicity. If you were ever to get caught again and tried to re-read the book, the information and the way in which it is presented would no longer be new. You would find yourself skipping pages thinking, 'Oh, I know that, I know that.' You would then reach the end of the book and say it doesn't work any more. The book never changes, only the way in which the person reading it perceives the words. This doesn't mean there isn't a possibility the book could work again if you fell back in, I am just saying don't risk it.

Your perception would be different because your brain would never read it the same way again, no matter how hard you tried. But why would you ever want to read this book again anyway? You would only ever need to pick up this book again if you were drinking alcohol again and why on earth would you ever want to do that?

This book is not a safety net, so do not use it as such. This is a key instruction. If you feel as though you need a safety net 'just in case' then, again, you have missed the point. Remember, just one drink will cost you over £100,000 and keep you as its slave for life. It will destroy you physically and mentally and affect your entire quality of life forever. See it for what it is and, that way, you cannot crave slavery, misery and the depletion of your mental and physical life. You can only jump for joy to be free.

You picked up this book and read it because you were, either consciously or subconsciously, looking for an escape from the alcohol trap. You have found one, so use it. Once you are free it would be ludicrous ever to go back again, especially when you know that it does nothing for you and that the chances of an easy and enjoyable escape the second time are virtually nil. So unlock that prison door, lock it behind you and throw away the key.

Alcohol addiction is an ingenious confidence trick and intelligent people do fall for them but what kind of person would ever fall for the same trick twice? Nobody, especially if they knew for certain that their life depended on it. The impact of this book would never be the same for you if you were to have just 'one' drink. Keep the book by all means. It can be a tool if you need to reverse any brainwashing should it start to creep in. Never underestimate the power of that insidious brainwashing. Counter it if you ever feel it rearing its ugly head but, if you do have just the 'one,' forget it; it's over.

I have written this book because I am adamant that I want to see an end to the completely unnecessary suffering alcohol causes its victims and society in general. I am committed to helping the world get free forever; not simply for a few weeks.

The world's perception of this drug will change but it will take time to change such an ingrained belief system. You will be an ambassador for that change. We are just at the beginning but, as your friend, I urge you always to enjoy your freedom and remember how lucky you are to be outside the prison. Keep it very clear in your mind that, no matter how long you have stopped, the grass is not greener on the other side. You already know that it isn't which is why you are reading this book. Do not look back through rose tinted glasses as the facts about alcohol addiction never change. The drug will always remain the same, no matter how long you have stopped drinking. It is a drug and that is why there is no such thing as one drink for anyone, not just you.

If you hit a moment of stress and someone offers you a drink, you need to understand that you are already stressed enough. The last thing you need is a lifelong addiction to add to your stress. More importantly, you will now know for certain that it would never resolve the stress; in fact, as with everything else, alcohol would do the exact opposite.

You were stuck in a mental prison. Now that you are free you should not think you have left anything behind. If you returned to look around the prison you would realise straight away that there was nothing there but by then it would be too late. As you turned to leave the door would shut tight and lock you in. The key to lifelong success is to imagine the prison with glass walls around it so that you can see that there is nothing inside long before you even contemplate having that one drink. Looking into the prison through glass walls is a great reminder of why you wanted to quit; why you wanted to escape. That way, once again, you will remind yourself of just how great it is to be free.

There are so many advantages to being free that you will simply have to discover them for yourself. However, the biggest gain for you is this:

You started this book thinking that you were different to everyone else; you can finish this book knowing you are. How exciting is that?

People come to my sessions full of doom and gloom. This is because society has established the rules that dictate they are different. Apparently these people should feel ashamed because they have fallen for the same confidence trick as the majority of the population. The problem is that, when they first join my sessions, they do feel ashamed. They have reached rock bottom and they come in feeling as though they are in a no-win situation. What they don't understand when they first arrive is that they are way ahead of the game. They have already realised they are trapped and, given the choice, they would love to escape. I help give them that choice. Within no time at all it begins to dawn on them that they are in exactly the same position as everybody else; hooked on a drug. They leave knowing they are not the same as everyone else, because they are no longer hooked. Once this has been understood, it is one of the best feelings in the world.

Thank you for sharing your time with me and having the courage to finish this book and make the very easy jump to freedom. You are achieving something truly amazing. Every time I hear of someone breaking free, I get tremendous satisfaction. I would love to hear from you. It would give me great pleasure to hear about your freedom and comments on your own experience. I may even meet you personally at one of my retreats in Turkey or Portugal. If, for whatever reason, we never do get the chance, I wish you a truly extraordinary life.

Best wishes

Jason Vale

If for whatever reason this book hasn't provided you with the freedom you were looking for, you may find a Jason Vale Ultimate Retreat useful. Jason conducts a few weeks a year at his health/fitness and addiction retreat in Portugal. Please see www.juicemaster.com for more details.